RACISM AND
PSYCHIATRY

Racism and Psychiatry

by ALEXANDER THOMAS, M.D.
and SAMUEL SILLEN, Ph.D.

BRUNNER/MAZEL, *PUBLISHERS* • NEW YORK
BUTTERWORTHS • LONDON

Second Printing

RACISM AND PSYCHIATRY

Copyright © 1972 by Alexander Thomas and Samuel Sillen
Published by
BRUNNER/MAZEL, INC.
64 University Place, New York, N. Y. 10003

Library of Congress Catalog Card No. 72-180788
SBN 87630-049-2

MANUFACTURED IN THE UNITED STATES OF AMERICA

Preface

WITH GROWING FORCE, the black liberation movement is shaking up traditional pieties and preconceptions in every sphere of American life. The mental health field is no exception. It has been undergoing a painful reassessment of its own role in perpetuating and reinforcing white racist attitudes and practices. The extent of such involvement has come as a shock to most white psychiatrists, psychologists, social workers, and other professionals. While they had long recognized that racism was endemic in our society, they had assumed that their special training and their dedication to humanistic values made them immune.

This was a grave miscalculation. It underestimated the tenacity of tradition, the deep roots of racist thinking in the history of the disciplines concerned with human behavior. The past was supposed to be safely buried; the most crude and blatant forms of prejudice had apparently been discredited many years ago. This assumption failed to reckon with the subtler formulations in which the same basic ideas now insinuate themselves. Overlooked too was the institutionalization of racism, the fact that oppression of black people was so thoroughly built into every social substructure.

In this book, we try to examine some of the ways in which white racism has influenced theory and practice in psychiatry and allied fields. The spur for such a revaluation is the recent work of a growing body of black psychiatrists, sociologists,

psychologists, and other scholars. Their initiative—both in
black caucuses at professional meetings and in publications—
has challenged every white worker in this field to take a fresh
look at long-standing presuppositions and ways of doing things.
Much of the thinking in these pages is indebted to their contributions, as will become clear. We should also note that an
impressive number of white professionals, especially younger
ones, are helping to demolish stereotypes that have long held
sway in this area. With these authors, we feel that it is the
responsibility of white psychiatrists not simply to deplore
racism, but to expose and eliminate it within their ranks.
While we focus here on discrimination against blacks, we are
of course aware that similar disadvantages are suffered by
other minorities, such as Mexican-Americans, Indians, and
Puerto Ricans.

   In committing himself to the struggle against a destructive
racism, the American psychiatrist can build on the examples
set by two towering figures of his profession: Benjamin Rush
and Harry Stack Sullivan. Rush, often called the "father of
American psychiatry," was a signer of the Declaration of In-
dependence and a strong opponent of slavery. He challenged
the belief that blacks are born inferior, asserting that white
claims of mental superiority are "founded alike in ignorance
and inhumanity" (Rush 1799). In our own century, Sullivan,
perhaps the most original and influential thinker that American
psychiatry has produced, showed a level of concern about
racism that was far ahead of the profession as a whole. During
the 1930's he worked with two pioneering black sociologists,
Charles S. Johnson and Franklin Frazier, on studies of black
youth in the South. Sharply critical of stereotypic and patronizing attitudes, Sullivan called upon psychiatrists to adopt a
non-exploiting approach to black Americans. "As a psychiatrist," he wrote, "I have to speak particularly against using
them as scapegoats for our unacceptable impulses; the fact
that they are dark-skinned and poorly adapted to our historic
puritanism is really too naive a basis for projecting most of

our privately condemned faults upon them. They deserve to be observed as they are, and the blot of an American interracial problem may thus gradually be dissipated" (Sullivan, 1964).

Unfortunately, the examples of Rush and Sullivan did not determine the main trends in psychiatric thinking. In the 19th and early 20th century, racist ideas were presented coarsely in both professional journals and popular press, as we shall detail in the first chapter, "Myths from the Past." In time such clumsy efforts to provide a scientific rationale for white supremacy became inadequate. They were made untenable by advances in the physical and social sciences. In their place we now have a host of more sophisticated concepts that buttress the ideology of racism. These range from arbitrary interpretation of IQ test findings to the theory that the ghetto's ills stem from the "fatherless" black family. They include the notion that the black psyche bears a "mark of oppression," a deformity of basic personality. They embrace such concepts as an instinctive and ineradicable aggression between races, "cultural deprivation," and racial fitness for learning by rote rather than conceptual thinking.

Many advocates of such views may sincerely disavow racism, and may even feel that their concepts further the struggle against racism. Our concern, however, is not with the intentions of individuals, but with the scientific validity and social consequences of their ideas. It is with these two issues in mind—validity and consequence—that currently prevailing views will be examined.

Contents

Preface v

Foreword by Kenneth B. Clark, Ph.D. xi

1. MYTHS FROM THE PAST 1

2. THE GENETIC FALLACY 23

3. "THE MARK OF OPPRESSION" 45

4. THE ILLUSION OF COLOR BLINDNESS 57

5. THE DEFICIENT "DEFICIT" MODEL 67

6. FAMILY AND FANTASY 83

7. THE SEXUAL MYSTIQUE 101

8. THE "SICKNESS" OF WHITE RACISM 112

9. PITFALLS OF EPIDEMIOLOGY 122

10. THE BLACK PATIENT: SEPARATE AND UNEQUAL 135

11. CHALLENGE TO THE PROFESSION 146

References 159

Index 171

Foreword

A CONSTANT FACTOR in the history of scientific progress seems
to be the unwillingness of certain individuals to accept the
prevailing assumptions or practices of a particular discipline
or profession. Such individuals are difficult to understand.
They are socialized in the same culture and are trained in the
same institutions as are their colleagues; nevertheless, they
refuse to follow the accepted dogmas and fashions of thought.
They are irritatingly creative because they dare to question
the unquestioned. Sometimes knowingly, but often without
seeming to have a choice, they invite the ridicule, criticisms,
even excommunication of their more traditional colleagues. In
daring to dissent, they arouse debates which cannot be successfully and permanently repressed. The power of their ideas
demands that these debates be resolved by evidence. Almost
always, this sequence of dissent, debate, gathering of evidence,
and verification, modification or refutation brings forth new
insights or new boundaries of knowledge and a more effective
technology.

Without regard to the consequences of their dissent, the
individuals who make such contributions to human knowledge
and social and personal ethical integrity are not initially wel-
comed by their scientific and professional colleagues. They are
viewed with suspicion and are likely to be treated as disloyal,
if not traitorous, members of the club. To raise serious questions and to doubt established practices—particularly in those

disciplines concerned with man's ego and his relation with his fellow man—is to invite personal jeopardy rather than professional reward. It is difficult to understand the source from which they derive the courage to dissent, to persist in their questioning, to insist upon new perspectives and approaches to old problems. We do not now have answers to these important questions—we can only speculate. All we do know is that these irritatingly questioning individuals are most valuable human beings. All human progress depends upon them and for this we must all be grateful to them.

In *Racism and Psychiatry*, my friend, Alexander Thomas, and his co-author, Samuel Sillen, confront their colleagues in the field of psychiatry and psychology with some profound scientific and moral questions. This book dares to dissect and analyze and expose to behavioral scientists and psychiatric professionals the subtle and flagrant forms of racism in the assumptions and practices of the science and profession. This book must be taken seriously by practitioners and by students. It is direct and clear in its indictment of the pervasive racism of psychiatric assumptions and practices. To say that this form of professional racism is not primary or peculiar to the behavioral sciences but is merely a reflection of the inescapable racism of the larger society does not ameliorate but compounds and makes more disturbing the moral scientific problem. Science in the latter third of the 20th Century must be an instrument of truth and justice; if it is not, it is an infernal accessory to dehumanization and death.

Probably the most disturbing insight obtained from the relentless clarity with which this book documents the case of racism in American psychiatry is the ironic fact that the students, research workers and professionals in the behavioral sciences—like members of the clergy and educators—are no more immune by virtue of their values and training to the disease and superstitions of American racism than is the average man. One must hope that this book would contribute to an acceptance of the scientific and moral responsibility of

psychologists and psychiatrists to help in freeing the human
mind of the constrictions of racial rejection and cruelty.

In writing this book, Dr. Thomas and Dr. Sillen have
made a valuable, a most important contribution to the social
and behavioral sciences. They have collected and analyzed
important research findings. They have brought their own
wisdom, sensitivities, and values to the analysis of current
controversies such as the Jensen assertions concerning the
genetically determined intellectual inferiority of Negroes. They
have drawn on their own observations and experiences as
sensitive clinicians, as systematic research scientists and as
empathic observers of the human predicament. They write
about the complex, multifaceted problems of racism and science as compassionate scholars. Their book is a model of the
imperative new dimension of contemporary science—the en-
meshment of respect for scientific objectivity and facts, a
permeating social sensitivity and an inescapable social responsibility for science, and a profound concern for the conservation of the unique positives of all human beings. With the
continued reinforcement of these inextricable ingredients, the
social and behavioral sciences of the present and the future
could contribute to the preservation rather than the oblitera-
tion of mankind.

KENNETH B. CLARK, PH.D.

Professor of Psychology, City College,
City University of New York;
President, Metropolitan Applied Research Center

RACISM AND
PSYCHIATRY

1
Myths from the Past

IN ITS LONG and ugly history in the United States, white racism has improvised a thousand variations on two basic themes. The first is that black people are born with inferior brains and a limited capacity for mental growth. The second is that their personality tends to be abnormal, whether by nature or by nurture. These concepts of inferiority and pathology are interrelated and reinforce each other. Both have served to sanctify a hierarchical social order in which "the Negro's place" is forever ordained by his genes and the accumulated disabilities of his past.

This view has a traditional corollary. It is that the black man functions best, psychologically, when he stays or is forcibly kept within the limits of his handicap. Unburdened by responsibility, he is cheerful and happy. Thrust into the competitive arena, he breaks down. Social tasks and privileges that are normal for white men are too stressful for him. Therefore, the racists argue, the best interests of both the black man himself and of the larger society dictate that his psychic impairment be recognized.

As proof of the black's predetermined deficiency, it was once considered sufficient to invoke Scriptural authority. According to Genesis, Noah was so enraged at his son Ham for beholding him naked that he thundered a curse dooming all the descendants of Ham to be the servants of servants. This

1

passage was interpreted with the customary latitude by plantation owners who identified their slaves with the doomed
tribe of Ham, thus providing unassailable Biblical support for
the thesis that blacks are inherently subordinate creatures.

But even in the days of slavery, white supremacists found
it expedient to unfurl the prestigious banner of science. They
measured a few crania and proclaimed that black people are
endowed by Nature with less gray matter. They cited figures
in the 1840 Census (fabricated, as we shall see) to prove that
blacks living under unnatural conditions of freedom in the
North were more prone to insanity. And they cited medical
testimony that presumably confirmed the physiological and
mental deviations of Negroes.

The black man, it was repeatedly claimed, was uniquely
fitted for bondage by his primitive psychological organization.
For him, mental health was contentment with his subservient
lot, while protest was an infallible symptom of derangement.
Thus a well-known physician of the ante-bellum South, Dr.
Samuel Cartwright of Louisiana, had a psychiatric explanation for runaway slaves. He diagnosed their malady as *drapetomania*, literally the flight-from-home madness, "as much a
disease of the mind as any other species of mental alienation."
Another ailment peculiar to black people was *dysaesthesia
Aethiopica,* sometimes called rascality by overseers, but actually due to "insensibility of nerves" and "hebetude of mind,"
explained Dr. Cartwright. Whereas psychologically normal
Negroes were faithful and happy-go-lucky, the mentally afflicted ones "pay no attention to the rights of property . . .
slight their work . . . raise disturbances with their overseers"
(Stampp, 1956).

The rationale for "scientific racism" leaned heavily on presumed racial differences in anatomy and physiology. The reported variations extended far beyond skin color or facial
features. Organic disparities ranged from body odor to speed
of nerve conduction. Influential medical journals presented the
crudest fantasies as if they were obvious facts. It was reported

in 1851 that the visible difference in skin pigmentation also characterized "the membranes, the muscles, the tendons, and all the fluids and secretions. Even the negro's brain and nerves, the chyle and all the humors, are tinctured with a shade of the pervading darkness." Dr. John S. Wilson of Georgia was one of the many physicians who contended that "the peculiarities in the disease of Negroes are so distinctive that they can be safely and successfully treated . . . only by Southern physicians" (Stampp, 1956). (This concept of the slavery era was to be echoed by a leading psychologist of a later generation, G. Stanley Hall [1905], who declared that medical treatment of the races was as different "as the application of veterinary medicine for horses is from that applied to oxen.")

The medical reports were blatantly contradictory. One physician asserted that the dominant characteristic of the Negro's physiology was the "blunted sensibility" of his nervous system, which enabled him to endure surgery better than white patients. Another doctor found that blacks showed a "fearful mortality" in surgery because they were lacking in "nervous endurance."

Needless to say, these constitutional differences—whether anatomical, neurological, or endocrinological—always represented a plus for the white man, a minus for the black. The existence of races, said the noted naturalist Louis Agassiz in 1850, "presses upon us the obligation to settle their relative rank" (Stanton, 1960). Agassiz met this self-imposed obligation, as did most of his contemporary scientists, by affirming the superior status of the Caucasian.

In ranking the races, the major yardstick used was the organ of thought. The Negro's brain, the racists asserted, is smaller and less developed than the white man's. This purported difference was cited as the physical basis of the psychological gulf between the races. The concept, harking back to the days of slavery, was embraced for many decades by most physicians and social scientists. It dovetailed with the prevailing 19th century view that psychological characteristics in general are determined by an inherited constitutional structure—the belief, for example, that criminal tendencies spring from a "bad seed."

2

A classical statement of the "primal difference" among races was elaborated in 1840 by Dr. Samuel G. Morton, a physician and professor of anatomy at Pennsylvania Medical College. Dr. Morton was a dedicated collector of crania. He measured the capacity of skulls by filling them with white pepper seed (he later used shot), and he became convinced by his craniometric research that the brain of the various races of man became "successively smaller" as one "descended" from the Caucasian to the Ethiopian (Stanton, 1960). The brain differential accounted for "those primeval attributes of mind, which, for wise purposes, have given our race a decided and unquestionable superiority over all the nations of the earth." Dr. Morton's finding was greeted and effectively publicized by another prominent physician of the time, Dr. Josiah Clark Nott of Mobile, Alabama, who announced that God had created the races as distinct species. This doctrine of diverse origins characterized the so-called American school of ethnology. Since this theory collided with the Biblical view that mankind has a common ancestor, an intense controversy ensued. Both sides, however, accepted the premise of black inferiority.

This medical and anthropological tradition that the black man's brain is inferior continued virtually undisturbed into the present century. In 1906, Dr. Robert Bennett Bean, a professor of anatomy at Johns Hopkins, published a learned article on "Some racial peculiarities of the Negro brain" in the *American Journal of Anatomy*. (To make sure that a larger public was not deprived of his findings, he published in the same year a popularized version in *Century Magazine*.) Dr. Bean enunciated a persuasive syllogism. The Negro's brain was smaller, he claimed, had fewer nerve cells and fibers; the brain's "efficiency" depends on the number and position of such fibers; hence "the possibilities of developing the Negro are limited" (Bean, 1906). The white man was endowed with determination, will power, self-control, "with a high development of the ethical and esthetic faculties and great reasoning powers." The black man loves melody and ostentation, lacks judgment, and is incapable of devising hypotheses. "We are forced to conclude," he said, "that it is useless to elevate the Negro by education or otherwise, except in the direction of his natural endowments."*

As it happened, the chairman of the anatomy department at Johns Hopkins, Franklin P. Mall, re-examined the specimens on which his colleague had based his conclusions and found no evidence whatsoever to support the claim of Caucasian superiority. In a detailed refutation of Bean, published in the *American Journal of Anatomy* three years later, Mall (1909) wrote: "For the present the crudeness of our method will not permit us to determine anatomical characters (of the human brain) due to race, sex and genius and which if they exist, are completely masked by the large number of individual variations. The study has been still further complicated by the personal equation of the investigator." Similar criticisms of Bean's findings had already been included in W. E. B. Du Bois' book, *The Health and Physique of the North American Negro*, published in 1906.

Despite the conclusive refutation of the racial "inferior brain" thesis by anthropologists and other scientists, notably Franz Boas, this myth is by no means dead. It crops up in new forms, and continually requires further refutation (Montagu, 1964; Harris, 1968b). In a detailed and careful review of the subject in the *American Journal of Physical Anthropology*, anatomist Phillip V. Tobias (1969) has effectively de-

---

* The phrase "We are forced to conclude" anticipates the token gesture of regret expressed by present-day authors who, like Bean, offer "scientific" evidence of black genetic inferiority.

molished the legend that there is a demonstrated correlation
between brain-size, gray matter, and race.

3

Another major tenet of "scientific racism," based on a superficial reading of Darwin, holds that various human groups
exist at different stages of biological evolution. The higher
races are those that have developed over a longer period of
time. On a lower rung of the ladder are those starters who
have not quite outgrown the handicaps of their simian past.
Eventually, it is presumed, they will climb to the perch now
occupied by the vanguard of mankind, who by then will have
moved on and still be out of reach. Since the theorists who
devised this scenario were white, it is not difficult to deduce
the skin color of the front-runners and of those who will pursue
them forever like figures on a Grecian urn.

According to this hypothesis, the younger races still have
juvenile minds. The development of every individual's psyche
recapitulates the history of his race from savagery to civilization. The "lower races" have less to recapitulate. Their mental
development terminates earlier, "in conformity with the biological law that the higher the organisms the longer they take
to evolve," said Herbert Spencer, one of the principal archi-
tects of this scheme. Spencer pointed out that the idea of
monogamy, for example, had been developed only by the
higher races, in whom it was now innate. In fact, said this
proper Victorian, a race's position on the evolutionary ladder
is indicated by its attitude toward marriage!

The phylogenetic concept of race was enormously influential. "Indeed, no major figure in the social sciences between
1860 and 1890 escaped the influence of evolutionary racism,"
notes a historian of anthropological theory. "Within anthropology this thralldom was not broken until the advent of the
Boasian movement; in adjacent disciplines, the struggle to
achieve a correct statement of the relationship between the

hereditary and learned components in sociocultural repertories has by no means been resolved" (Harris, 1968b).

In psychology and psychiatry, the assumptions of phylogenetic thinking were long pervasive. One of the most influential proponents of the concept was "the father of child study" in this country, G. Stanley Hall, founder of the *American Journal of Psychology* in 1887 and first president of the American Psychological Association. In his autobiography, *Life and Confessions of a Psychologist*, Hall describes his achievement in making his contemporaries more aware that "every child, from conception to maturity, recapitulates every stage of development through which the human race from its lowest animal beginning has passed."* Hall believed that the child must be permitted to work out his vestigial compulsions specific to each phylogenetic stage (savage, barbarian, nomadic wanderer, etc.), or else the repressed demands would later assert themselves in a distorted form. Certain primitive races, like children, are in a state of immature development and must be treated gently and understandingly by more developed peoples. Thus, in his widely read work, *Adolescence* (1904), Hall described Africans, Indians, and Chinese as members of "adolescent races" in a stage of incomplete growth. This theory is obviously linked to the "White Man's Burden" so benevolently assumed by Rudyard Kipling and his imperialist contemporaries in relation to the "lesser breeds" and the "half devil, half child" natives of non-European countries.

As president of Clark University, Hall brought Freud to America to attend that school's twentieth anniversary in 1909. While Freud did not share his host's racist notions, several of his American followers did, as is abundantly evident in

---

* One is reminded of Freud's dictum that "each individual repeats in some abbreviated fashion during childhood the whole course of the development of the human race" (Freud, 1953).

The recapitulation theory of mental development was searchingly examined as far back as 1913 by E. L. Thorndike, who concluded that "the influence which it has exerted upon students of human nature is due, not to rational claims, but to its rhetorical attractiveness."

their contributions to *The Psychoanalytical Review*. This journal, the first psychoanalytical periodical in English, was founded in 1913 by two leading American psychiatrists, William Alanson White and Smith Ely Jeliffe. The first volume carried three articles dealing with mental illness among blacks, as well as a note by the editors declaring that "The existence side by side of the white and colored races in the United States offers a unique opportunity not only to study the psychology of a race at a relatively low cultural level, but to study their mutual effects upon one another." In availing themselves of this "unique opportunity," *The Psychoanalytical Review* authors applied a thin coating of psychiatric jargon to standard myths about race, including the phylogenetic fantasy.

Painful as it is to read these articles, one must face up to the task if one is to comprehend the level of racist thought that dominated American psychiatry for a good part of its history, as it did other scientific and professional disciplines.

One of the articles, "Dementia Praecox in the Colored Race," was contributed by Arrah B. Evarts, a physician at the Government Hospital for the Insane in Washington, D. C. "It is a fact recognized by all that the individual in his development relives the history of the race," the article begins. "Upon this fact is built one of the fundamental principles of pedagogy: that a child should be allowed to develop in sympathy with his race trend. It is also fundamental to the full understanding of psychiatry. Again and again do we see an individual struggling against the awful onslaught of a psychosis, reverting to progressively lower and lower strata of the formation of his race." Therefore, in order to understand dementia praecox in blacks, one must study their race history. Dr. Evarts' own source of enlightenment in this respect was Theodore Roosevelt's self-glorifying account of his African safari on which he met "strong, patient, childlike savages" and "happy-go-lucky porters," superstitious, bereft of a moral sense but who do have a great "compensating gift," music: "They all sing." And since the American explorer's descriptions of "darkest" Africa echoed all the stereotypes about the blacks back home, what could be clearer than the continuity of racial personality? In view of the black man's background it is "miraculous," Dr. Evarts asserts, that in America he has gone as far as he has: "All honor to the race which has accomplished the impossible," thanks to his bondage, which "in reality was a wonderful aid to the colored man. The necessity for mental initiative was never his, and his racial characteristic of imitation carried him far on the road."

But not far enough to overcome his psychiatric disability. "During its years of savagery," Dr. Evarts continues, "the race has learned no lessons in emotional control, and what they attained during their few generations of slavery left them unstable. For this reason we find deterioration in the emotional sphere most often an early and a persistent manifestation. . . . Because the colored patient already lives upon a plane much lower than his white neighbor, actual deterioration in the individual must be differentiated from the supposed loss of a racial period he has not yet attained." The history of the race makes it peculiarly prone to dementia praecox, but psychiatrists must be careful to distinguish between the psychotic behavior of blacks and whites. Since the ability to stick to a task is "already deficient in the race," the impairment of staying power may be more apparent than real. Since sexual instincts are unrestrained, there are fewer sexual perversions, and a female masturbator is rare on colored wards. Buried complexes do not seem to exist, but "Dementia praecox is dementia praecox still, though present in an already primitive race." While Dr. Evarts presents some superficial case studies, it is clear that his observations are basically determined by racist preconceptions rather than a fresh look at the evidence.

A second article in Volume I of *The Psychoanalytical Review*, "The Dream as a Simple Wish-Fulfillment in the Negro," was contributed by John E. Lind, a colleague of Dr. Evarts at the Government Hospital for the Insane. According to Dr. Lind, the American student of psychology has a unique advantage in having ready "access" to a race "which furnishes numerous individuals showing psychological aspects quite similar to those of the savage." The minds of blacks, "especially the so-called pure-blooded Negro," are less complex than those of Caucasians; therefore their dreams must also be "simpler in type." As authority for this deduction, Lind cited Freud's statement that children's dreams are simpler than those of adults inasmuch as their psychic activities are less complicated. In this connection, Freud said in *The Interpretation of Dreams* that "Child psychology, in my opinion, is destined to render the same services to the psychology of adults as a study of the structure or development of the lower animals renders to the investigation of the structure of the higher orders of animals." While the analogy drawn by Freud is open to question, it is clear that he was not talking about lower and higher races. But his American follower, imbued with the concept that blacks represent the childhood stage of mankind's development, translated Freud's observation into racist terms. Nor was Dr. Lind, unfortunately, the last to do so.

To verify Freud's theory that the dreams of children are simple fulfillments of wishes, writes Dr. Lind, "I obtained the dreams of one hundred Negroes, selecting only those who were pure-blooded to the best of the information obtainable on the subject." Evidently, as a conscientious scientist, Dr. Lind was at pains to avoid contaminating his sample with genes for white psychic complexity. And his prudence paid off, since no fewer than 84 of his 100 had wish-fulfillment dreams of a "juvenile" character.

Since he gives several examples, we may judge for ourselves. An 87-year-old black man said, "I dreamed I was going to get my pension." The psychiatrist comments: "This dreamer has for years been endeavoring to obtain a pension from the government, although he has no actual disability to entitle him to such." Now what could be more childish? A 25-year-old laborer, spending his eighth day in jail, awaiting sentence for assault, said, "I dreamed I was out. The police went one way and I went another." This is classified as "retrospective wish-fulfillment." A 23-year-old man who had been in jail 110 days and had seven more days to go: "I dreamed I was out for a good time with the girls." Since these dreams were frank expressions of wish-fulfillment and did not show the distorting activities of an inner censor, the black dreamers plainly reflect a "primitive type of mind." As white American psychiatrists, then, we have a clear advantage over foreigners like Freud: "Although Freud has recommended the study of child psychology as a valuable aid to the understanding of abnormal adult psychology, it must be remembered that in his country there is no such race as we have here whose psychological processes are simple in character and so readily obtainable. Perhaps to the American investigator, the Negro might prove as valuable and more accessible than the child."

Lest anyone get the impression that such psychiatric balderdash was pre-empted by *The Psychoanalytical Review,* we may turn to Volume I, Number 1 of the *American Journal of Psychiatry* (July, 1921). Here the phylogenetic theme is sounded by Dr. W. M. Bevis of St. Elizabeths Hospital in Washington, D. C. His paper is on "Psychological Traits of the Southern Negro with Observations as to Some of His Psychoses." True to form, the opening sentence declares: "The Negro race evinces certain phylogenetic traits of character, habit, and behavior that seem sufficiently important to make the consideration of these peculiarities worthwhile; especially as these psychic characteristics have their effect upon and are reflected in the psychoses most frequently seen in the Negro." Then follows the dreary procession of stereotypes: "All Negroes have a fear of darkness . . . careless, credulous, childlike, easily amused, sadness and depression have little part in his psychic make-up," . . . and so on, and so on, cluttering the pages of the nation's leading psychiatric journal with racist clichés. The psychiatrist especially emphasizes the black man's talent for mimicry, with which he tries to "compensate for psychic inferiority by imitating the white race. . . . Efforts to imitate his white neighbors in speech, dress, and social customs are often overwrought and ludicrous, but sometimes sufficiently exact to delude the uninitiated into the belief that the mental level of the Negro is only slightly inferior to that of the Caucasian."

Dr. Bevis reported that Negro children are bright and full of life, but their mental development starts freezing at puberty. From then on theirs is a life of sexual promiscuity, gambling, petty thievery, drinking, loafing, and the rest of the familiar catalogue. This prodigal life, dictated by racial inheritance, produces a host of mental diseases. At the top in frequency stands dementia praecox. "This is not surprising when their racial character make-up and the atmosphere of superstition in which they move are considered. Much of their usual behavior seems only a step from the simpler types of this classification."

Even more crude, if possible, is an article on "Psychoses in the Colored Race: A Study in Comparative Pychiatry" by still another physician at the Government Hospital for the Insane, Dr. Mary O'Malley. Published in 1914 in the *American Journal of Insanity* (forerunner of the *American Journal of Psychiatry*), this article was cited for years in the psychiatric literature (by Bevis too, of course) as an authoritative study. Its scientific pretensions were impressive, since it professed to be based on a study, conducted from 1909 to 1914, of 880 women patients (455 white, 345 black). But as one examines the article, it turns out to be a confession of ignorance. The black patients, most of whom were former slaves or the descendants of slaves in Maryland and Virginia, evidently didn't open their minds for Dr. O'Malley. "There is little known of the psychology of these people. . . . The colored are secretive by nature as well as by cultivation. . . . It requires a great amount of painstaking effort and hours of toil to obtain any conception of the mechanisms of the Negro mind."

Yet certain truths about that mind were self-evident *a priori*. Deficiencies in "evolutional advancement" had produced racial peculiarities that determined special types of mental reaction. The psychiatrist felt that this was all so plain that it needed no explanation for an intelligent professional readership. "A psychosis in an obviously lower race, such as the colored race really is, must necessarily offer some features from a mental standpoint which distinguish it in a general way from a psychosis in a higher race. This is so apparent that it requires no further discussion. The lower psychic development of the colored race, under certain pathological conditions, offers some phenomena which are observed to approach more nearly the general features and characteristics of children."

Out of harmony with a higher stage of civilization than nature had prepared them for, blacks develop mental disorder as "a compensatory defense." But only certain kinds of disorders. Not depression, which might argue a certain level of "evolutional advancement" in sensitivity. But psychiatry, with its phylogenetic orientation, could offer the blacks one consolation. Since they had not climbed to the same evolutionary heights as the Caucasians, they did not have the same depth of reversion. They had less backsliding to do when they became mentally ill. And so they did not reach the degraded condition of white patients, Dr. O'Malley explained. Under the same circumstances they were "not as filthy and disgusting," less given to expose their person, and less likely to soil or wet themselves. But this did not, the psychiatrist hastily added, make them trustworthy.

Among the famous European psychiatrists, the one who most fancied himself as an expert on blacks was Carl Gustav Jung, who on one of his visits to America examined some black patients in a mental hospital. "If you study races as I have done," declared the Swiss analyst, "you can make very interesting discoveries." But his discoveries merely echo the stereotypes of his American contemporaries. Like them he believed that "The different strata of the mind correspond to the his-

tory of the races" and that the Negro "has probably a whole
historical layer less" than the white man. Jung found that
black "primitiveness" has infected American behavior in general. "What is more contagious than to live side by side with
a rather primitive people?" he asked. Jung saw the influence
of "the childishness of the Negro," not all of it unfavorable,
he conceded, in everything from the swaying of American
hips to the "inimitable Rooseveltian laugh" (Jung, 1928, 1930).
Jung also explained the "energetic sexual repressions" of
Americans as a defensive maneuver against blacks. "The
causes for the repression," Jung explained at the Second Psychoanalytic Congress in 1910, "can be found in the specific
American Complex, namely to the living together with lower
races, especially with Negroes. Living together with barbaric
races exerts a suggestive effect on the laboriously tamed instinct of the white race and tends to pull it down. Hence, the
need for strongly developed defensive measures, which precisely show themselves in those specific features of American
culture" (quoted by Brill in Freud, 1938).

We may now shake our heads in amazement that such
crude racist formulations were believed implicitly by readers
of the most prestigious psychiatric journals. But rather than
feel superior to the benighted psychiatrists of past generations,
we should be reminded how easy it is to distort science in the
service of racism.

4

Racist theorizers have also traditionally invoked the concept of "instinct" to support their claim of inborn psychological differences and antagonisms between human populations.
The term "instinct" in its promiscuous career has embraced
a multitude of speculations about inherited behavior patterns.
One scholar who surveyed the psychological and social science
literature counted up some 14,000 alleged instincts (Bernard,
1924). That was nearly 50 years ago, and the number would
no doubt be even more impressive today. Truly, as Gordon

Allport (1961) once observed, "It is easy to invent instincts according to one's need."

The instinct postulate offers a seductively simple explanation for the most complex human phenomena. Wars are said to stem from man's "instinct of aggression," private fortunes from the "instinct of acquisition," and political dictatorships from the "instinct of domination." As evidence that such inborn drives exist, the instinctivists point to the recurrence of wars, greed, and power grabs. Understandably, this circular argument has had a special attraction for defenders of things as they are. For if our behaviors are predetermined by powerful instinct, it would appear futile to strive for basic social change.

This concept became a major weapon in the racist armamentarium. The most ardent of instinct psychologists, William McDougall, was also one of the most vocal racist theorizers. McDougall's influential *Introduction to Social Psychology* (1908), which went through some 25 editions, elaborated a battery of instincts that included, among others, possessiveness, pugnacity, hunting, kindness, teasing, bullying, cleanliness, adornment, and superstition. To this catalog McDougall added the "instinct of submission." And he confidently asserted that "in the great strength of this instinct of submission, we have the key to the history of the Negro race" (McDougall, 1921). As an illustration, he cited the story of a black woman worker whose "mistress," after treating her shortcomings with great forbearance for a time, suddenly scolded her. The black "maid," rather than showing resentment, expressed relief and exclaimed, "Lor', Missus, you do make me feel so good." With this "typical and significant" anecdote the distinguished professor of psychology at Harvard demonstrated conclusively that black people have an instinctive need to be pushed around by white people.

The instinct hypothesis was also pressed into service to account for conflict between the races. As one president of the American Sociological Society put it, color prejudice is

"the instinctive expression of a sense of cultural difference
and social status" (Weatherly, 1910). Unfortunately the notion of "instinctive dislike" was not limited to blatant racists.
Sociologist W. I. Thomas of the University of Chicago developed a theory of "consciousness of kind" which held that race
prejudice "is an instinct originating in the tribal stage of
society . . . (it) will probably never disappear completely"
(Thomas, 1904). This instinct was said to provoke a reflex
of repulsion at the mere sight of physical features different
from those of the beholder. As one student of anti-black
thought in America has noted (Newby, 1965): "With no intention of doing so, Thomas had provided rational and scientific justification for racial discrimination and segregation. He
had made more plausible the assertion that Southern race policies were expressions of biological law and racial instinct
rather than bigotry and prejudice." As a result, Southern Congressmen could declare that lynch mobs were merely answering
the "call of the blood."*

5

Still another curious chapter in the history of racism in
psychiatry was the misuse of statistics to provide a scientific
facade for dehumanizing black people. Epidemiology, the
branch of medicine that studies the frequency and distribution of disease in a population, was long ago manipulated to
buttress one of the main psychiatric arguments in support of
slavery—the claim that the black man becomes prey to mental
disturbance when he is set free. Clear evidence for this con-

---

* Later, the Nazi philosophers of instinct and the "call of the
blood" were fond of quoting the report in Houston Stewart Chamberlain's *The Foundations of the Nineteenth Century* (1911): "It frequently happens that children who have no conception of what 'Jew'
means, or that there is any such thing in the world, begin to cry as
soon as a genuine Jew or Jewess comes near them!" To Chamberlain,
this demonstration of instinctual aversion was worth more than "a
whole anthropological congress." The instinctivists never bothered to
explain why, in light of the inborn repugnance between ethnic groups,
it was necessary to enact drastic laws forbidding intermarriage.

tention seemed to be provided by the Sixth U.S. Census of 1840, the first federal census that attempted to enumerate mentally diseased and defective persons. The census showed that the rate of "insanity and idiocy" among Negroes was 11 times higher in the North than in the South. The incidence of black madness in the slave states was only 1 in 1,558 compared to 1 in 162.4 in the free states. The ratio of insanity between Negroes and whites in the North was 6 to 1, whereas it was 3 to 5 in the South. And the discrepancy appeared to widen with the geographical latitude. While 1 one of every 14 Negroes in Maine was a "madman," only 1 out of 4,310 was so afflicted in Louisiana.

Pro-slavery apologists eagerly seized upon such figures as scientific confirmation of the black man's natural inferiority. "Here is proof of the necessity of slavery," asserted John C. Calhoun. "The African is incapable of self-care and sinks into lunacy under the burden of freedom. It is a mercy to give him the guardianship and protection from mental death."* This theme was amplified in numerous speeches and tracts, North and South (Litwack, 1961).

One of those who at first accepted the 1840 Census figures at face value was Dr. Edward Jarvis, a Massachusetts physician and specialist in mental disorders. Apparently, he concluded, slavery shielded the Negro "from some of the liabilities and dangers of active self-direction." But Dr. Jarvis had a passion for statistics (he later served as president of the American Statistical Association for 31 years), and when he took a closer look at the figures he found that the census was a "fallacious and self-condemning document" (Jarvis, 1844). It turned out that many of the Northern towns credited with mentally deranged Negroes had no black inhabitants at all! Lily-white Scarsboro, Maine, had been assigned six insane Negro inhabitants. Worcester, Massachusetts, was alleged to

---

* In 1844, as Secretary of State, Calhoun cited the 1840 Census figures to justify the annexation of Texas and the extension of slavery.

have 133 Negro lunatics and idiots, but the figure was the
number of patients, all white, at the Worcester State Hospital
for the insane.* The 165 black cases listed for Ohio included
88 that were distributed among towns containing only 31
Negroes. Similar inventions characterized the list in state after
state, resulting in what one modern student called "one of the
most amazing tissues of statistical falsehood and error ever
woven together under government imprint" (Deutsch, 1944).

After exposing the fabrication in a medical journal, Dr.
Jarvis persuaded the Massachusetts Medical Society to demand a correction of the census. Black people were outraged
by the distortion, and a mass meeting of Negroes in New
York petitioned the U.S. Senate to re-examine and revise the
figures (Morais, 1967).* "Freedom has not made us mad, it
has strengthened our minds by throwing us upon our own
resources," wrote a leading black physician, Dr. James Mc-
Cune Smith, to the New York *Tribune*. And Representative
John Quincy Adams pressed for a Congressional investigation.

A response to the critics came from Secretary of State
Calhoun (whose department was then in charge of the census).
He told Adams that "where there were so many errors, they
balanced one another, and led to the same conclusion as if

---

* Actually, most asylums in the North excluded blacks—for example, the Indiana Hospital for the Insane did not take Negroes on the
ground that they were not legal citizens of the state, a practice de-
nounced as inhumane by Dr. James Athon, superintendent of the institution (Dain, 1964). During the Civil War, Dr. Samuel Gridley
Howe, who headed the Freedman's Inquiry Commission, queried all
asylum superintendents in the Union about the number of insane
Negroes in their states and learned that in the few asylums that
sometimes admitted Negroes the ratio was one to several thousand
white patients. Dr. John S. Butler, superintendent of the Hartford
Retreat, attributed the small number of blacks in his institution to
their constitutional cheerfulness, which made them less vulnerable to
insanity. The Northern psychiatrists "did not seem to see the contradiction in ascribing the lack of Negroes in their hospitals to their
alleged general immunity to the disease and at the same time admit-
ting that hospitals did not ordinarily admit Negroes" (Dain, 1964).

* The text of this petition is in Morais' *The History of the Negro
in Medicine*.

they were all correct." (This argument ignored the fact that the errors went in only one direction.) When an official investigation was finally undertaken, Calhoun appointed William A. Weaver, a Southerner who had been superintendent of the 1840 Census, to investigate himself. To nobody's surprise, Weaver concluded that the errors had not been committed. And so the figures remained in the government books, to be cited for many years in the psychiatric literature. "Who would believe," asked a writer in the *American Journal of Insanity* in 1851, "without the fact in black and white before him, that every fourteenth colored person in the State of Maine is an idiot, or a lunatic?" This question prompted Dr. Jarvis (1852) to remind readers of the journal that the "facts" had long ago been exposed as fabrications.*

Dr. Jarvis' words on this occasion are worth repeating because they describe so eloquently a public attitude that has by no means vanished. "It has seemed somewhat remarkable," he wrote in 1852, "that statements so glaringly false in themselves, so palpably contradictory to each other, so contrary to all common observations and experience, so unsupported by any analogies or even theories, should have been so passively acquiesced in by the people of this country, and especially by the naturalists, the physicians and the statisticians of America. . . . After all this indifference on the part of the public authorities who assumed the responsibility of this document, and the apathy and neglect on the part of the medical profession, who ought to know and look after these things, and who should jealously watch over the reports of science and natural history of our country, it is not strange that the people believed these new statements,—that newspaper writers, not familiar with nosological science, should repeat and publish these 'startling facts,' and that the world should trem-

---

* As an example of the far-reaching influence of the 1840 Census, it is of interest that a French author of a work on medicine and geography used its figures to prove that "cold vitiates the mental health of the Negro."

ble at the very thought of the overwhelming power of lunacy upon the colored race, when left to itself, in the free States of this Union."

In the Reconstruction and post-Reconstruction periods, statistical evidence was again adduced, this time to demonstrate that mental illness among blacks had sharply increased following Emancipation. The reason seemed perfectly clear to reputable psychiatrists, who pointed out that black people were now deprived of the care and supervision and restraining influences of ante-bellum days (Witmer, 1891; Babcock, 1895). In 1887 an international medical congress heard a report that the proportionate increase of insanity among Negroes was far greater than in any other group in the American population. From 1870 to 1880, it was claimed, the black population had increased about 35%, while the number of insane among them had risen 285%. "The causes," said the reporter, J. B. Andrews, "are briefly told: enlarged freedom, too often ending in license; excessive use of stimulants; excitement of the emotions, already unduly developed; the unaccustomed strife for means of subsistence; educational strain and poverty" (Andrews, 1887).

For decades such wildly inflated figures were cited to emphasize that freedom was pathogenic for the black man because it violated his natural need for submissiveness to authority. The 1840 Census figures were revived to show that Negroes were relatively free of mental illness in the slavery days. But the ante-bellum picture is less idyllic when one examines the inventory and appraisement records of Southern estates. These records indicate that the reporting of mental illness by the slaveholders was grossly inaccurate. "It was essential for the profitable management of the plantation that everyone who could be employed be assigned some gainful task," notes Postell (1953). "The planter soon found that many suffering from some nervous or mental disorder could be taught a simple routine and thus could be profitably employed. . . . From an economic point of view these Negroes were earning their living and were therefore not to be considered 'insane or idiotic.' " Slaves listed as "unsound" were often appraised at almost their full value. When the black man ceased to be property there was no reason why he should not be listed as defective, and every deviation from the white man's way of thinking and doing was then described as a pathologic sign. Thus the contention that there had been a precipitous rise in mental illness as a result of freedom was based on statistics without substance.

Paralleling the claim that emancipation unbalanced the Negro's mind was the contention that it jeopardized his body. For decades after the Civil War, medical journals carried reports of a basic change taking place in the black man's physiological makeup. The gradual extinction of the race was predicted as an "unerring certainty" by physicians North and South. This belief in the Negro's inevitable physical decline became "one of the most pervasive ideas in American medical and anthropological thought during the late nineteenth century" (Haller, 1970b)—an ironical counterpoint to current racist predictions that black fertility will overwhelm the country.

Partly the "extinction" thesis reflected wishful thinking; partly it was based on faulty analyses of the federal censuses; but mainly it served as further evidence of the black man's incompetence to get along without a white master. It was another manifestation of the systematic humiliation which W. E. B. Du Bois described in 1897, "the cynical ignoring of the better and boisterous welcoming of the worse, the all-pervading desire to inculcate disdain for everything black."

The theory of physical decline, like that of psychological breakdown, assumed that the blacks had flourished under slavery, a myth long perpetuated in story and song. "The slave of tradition was a physically robust specimen who suffered from few of the ailments which beset the white man. A tradition with less substance to it has seldom existed" (Stampp, 1956). According to this tradition, the master, whether out of kindness or self-interest, saw to it that his chattels were well fed, adequately clothed, and given proper medical treatment. But the reality was quite different. Pellagra, beriberi, and scurvy were rampant. The diaries of plantation owners themselves were filled with lamentations about workdays lost when fierce epidemics struck: "All the plagues of Egypt still infest these Negroes." And as Solomon Northup, a fugitive slave, noted in his autobiography, no black man on a cotton plantation was "ever likely to suffer from the gout, superinduced by excessive high living."

2

The Genetic Fallacy

TWO THOUSAND YEARS AGO, the Roman orator Cicero advised a friend: "Do not obtain your slaves from Britain because they are so stupid, and so utterly incapable of being taught." A thousand years later, the Moorish savant Said of Toledo observed: "Races north of the Pyrenees are of cold temperament and never reach maturity; they are of great stature and of a white color. But they lack all sharpness of wit and penetration." In the modern era, "innate" qualities have been ascribed to various groups: the "indolent" Irish, the "clannish" Italians, the "cunning" Jews, the "fickle" Japanese. It would appear that we all inhabit glass houses, but this has not restrained our common proclivity to throw stones.

The belief that human populations differ in their inherited mental qualities has been one of the basic premises of racist thought. The specific formulation of this genetic doctrine varies in sophistication from period to period, but the essence is always the same. Some races are said to inherit a capacity for abstract thought, others for learning only by rote; some are equipped to exercise foresight, while others are fated to be creatures of impulse. Such differences are unalterable, whether one views them as "in the blood" or "encoded in the genes."

For the white racist, the genetic argument offers an apparently scientific basis for viewing blacks as inferior. Since

23

blacks and whites inherit different physical characteristics such as skin color and hair texture, why not different psychic structures? The next step is to assert that the intellectual potential of blacks is genetically limited, as compared with whites. To recognize this presumed fact is "objectivity," to deny it is "sentimentalism."

The dominant assumption in 19th- and early 20th-century writings is epitomized in an influential book, *The Psychology of Peoples,* by the French physician and sociologist Gustave Le Bon (1898). He divided mankind into various groups on the basis of psychological traits, with the white Indo-Europeans occupying a higher rank than Negroes, Chinese, Japanese, and the Semitic peoples. A "mental abyss" separated the races, Le Bon maintained, and ineradicable differences in their genetic endowment determined the nature of their societies. "The various elements of the civilization of a people being only the outward signs of its mental constitution, the expression of certain modes of feeling and thinking peculiar to a people, these elements cannot be transmitted unchanged to peoples of a different mental constitution; all that can be transmitted is the exterior, superficial, and unimportant forms."*

As applied to blacks, this belief in the inheritance of racial psychology was omnipresent in the United States for generations. It was typified at the turn of the century by Nathaniel S. Shaler (1890), head of Harvard's Lawrence Scientific School (and son of a Kentucky slaveholder). "Men of science have at length found a clue to unravel the mysteries which surround the matter of human relations," Shaler exulted. "The

---

* The classic racist work of the 19th century was Count de Gobineau's *Essay on the Inequality of Human Races* (1853-1857), which the Nazis were to adopt as an authority for their doctrine of "Aryan" or "Nordic" supremacy. Before the Nazis, American racists (for example, Madison Grant in *The Passing of the Great Race,* 1916) had popularized in this country Gobineau's view that the hope of civilization rested on people of Northern European stock, who alone had an inherited "instinct for order," "perseverance," "love of liberty," "reflective energy," and, not least to be sure, "honor."

knowledge of the laws of inheritance, one of the affirmed triumphs of modern biology, has led us to understand the extent to which the conduct of men is determined by the habits of their ancestors." Shaler found that the Negro was "indelibly marked" by the indolent characteristics of his forefathers raised in the tropics, while the Caucasians, descended from folk who braved northern winter's trials, had a "precious heritage of energy and foresight which has given them the mastery of the world." This argument for white domination was based on the notion that acquired characteristics are inherited, a theory that turned out to be not one of the "triumphs" of biology but a mockery.*

Such genetic formulations gradually lost influence as evidence accumulated that behavioral characteristics previously labeled hereditary in origin were actually determined by life experiences. The main ground for arguing black racial inferiority has shifted from physical inheritance to social experience. That is, the onus is now placed on the history of oppression suffered by black people and the early life experiences of the individual black. (We shall deal with "the mark of oppression," "cultural deprivation," "pathological family," and similar concepts in later chapters.)

However, this does not mean that the genetic argument is a dead one. Far from it!

While most professionals may not favor the theory of inherited psychological inferiority, it remains a standard way of thinking among laymen. People tend to explain individual characteristics in terms of their being "in the blood." Furthermore, even among professional workers there has been an attempt to pump fresh life into the genetic concepts. The most recent example is the work of educational psychologist Arthur

---

* The important role of neo-Lamarckian ideas in late 19th-century thought is discussed by Stocking (1968), who notes that Lamarckianism "had much to do with determining the character of the prevailing racialism. Furthermore, in the context of 'Social Darwinism' it helped to legitimitize in *biological* terms the causal efficacy of *social* processes."

Jensen, whose theory that blacks are born with lower intelligence than whites will be examined in a moment.

2

What can a scientific approach tell us about the notion of inborn racial inferiority?

To begin with, the concept of race itself is not a settled issue. Ever since the pioneering work of Boas, leading anthropologists have sharply challenged the traditional assumptions. Ashley Montagu (1964), for example, considers race to be an "utterly erroneous and meaningless" concept in the light of modern genetics, as well as socially harmful. The term "race," he argues, should be dropped from the anthropologist's vocabulary as "phlogiston" was abandoned by chemists and "instinct" by many psychologists. The division of mankind into distinct races (ranging from a handful to hundreds, depending on the classifier) originated not in nature but in 18th-century thought as a convenience for grouping people with observable differences in skin color or hair texture. While there are differences in the distribution of some genes among various populations, "race" obfuscates the nature of these differences and reads arbitrary meanings into them. The concept represents an artificial "averaging" that ignores intragroup differences as well as overlapping between populations. "Physical type, heredity, blood, culture, nation, personality, intelligence, and achievement are all stirred together to make an omelet which is the popular conception of 'race.' "

Similar criticisms have been advanced by other leading anthropologists. Livingstone (1962) maintains that there are no races but only gradients in measurable genetic characters within the human species. The biological variation between population is continuous and "does not conform to the discrete packages labelled races." Or, as Washburn (1963) puts it: "Since races are open systems which are intergrading, the number of races will depend on the purpose of the classification."

Recent findings in population genetics emphasize the need

for caution against any easy assumption of common genetic characteristics for all members of even an apparently distinct population group. A leading investigator (Neel, 1970) underscores "the new humility incumbent upon us all" in light of the latest biochemical techniques used in genetic research. For example, a study of South American Indians shows a remarkable degree of genetic differences among members of the same tribe, even though the term "tribe" suggests a rather homogeneous grouping. "It is becoming increasingly clear," says Neel, "that the breeding structure of real populations—especially those that approximate the conditions under which man evolves—departs so very far from the structure subsumed by the classical formulations of population genetics that new formulations may be necessary before the significance of this variation can be appraised by mathematical means."

The confusion generated by simplistic approaches is compounded by the use of a common racial label for individuals who have markedly different backgrounds. Simply designating a group as racially distinct does not by fiat give its members common genetic characteristics. This error is evident in the indiscriminate lumping of two nonidentical concepts: social race and biological race (Harris, 1968a). In popular usage, the term "race" is applied to a great variety of groupings: tribes, nation-states, language families, ethnic minorities, groups that look distinct but are genetically mixed. Social race is determined by legal decree, group membership, consciousness of identity, genealogical relationships. Racial classification in the United States is governed by a social fiction: children of unions between blacks and whites are identified as blacks, with no recognition of the biological fact that they receive half of their hereditary endowment from each parent.

All of these considerations highlight the dangers of making inferences as to genetic causes of observed behavioral differences between population groups. As anthropologist Marvin Harris (1968a) points out, "One of the most common methodological blunders in scientific studies of the significance of racial differences in the United States is the tacit acceptance of this phantasmic notion of race as the basis for establishing research samples." This problem is abundantly evident in the medical and psychological literature.

Additional warnings against generalizations about racial characteristics come from the field of behavioral genetics, which has attracted growing interest in the decade since the pioneering textbook by Fuller and Thompson (1960). To what extent are observed differences in the behavior of individuals and groups inherited? The method of behavior-genetic analysis rejects the old dichotomy between nature and nurture. It recognizes, instead, the complex interaction of the specific genetic endowment and the specific environment that produces the observable characteristic. A gene does not express itself in isolation from a particular set of circumstances. Even where a simple characteristic is involved, such as height, the manifestation of the genetic influence is inseparably bound up with the nutritional state of the organism. How much more intricate is the process involving complex behavioral traits, such as "intelligence." "The expression of any gene depends on the prevailing genetic background, the prevailing environmental conditions, and their many possible interactions," notes Jerry Hirsch (1967), a prominent authority in the field of behavior genetics. Human development is not simply an unfolding of genetic structures, but a cumulative process of interaction.

When one considers the genetic diversity of mankind and the unique genetic endowment of each individual at conception (except for identical twins), when one remembers that the number of genes runs into many thousands, and that the number of potential environments is beyond count, it would appear most hazardous to generalize about racially inherited behavioral traits.

But even if one assumes greater genetic homogeneity than actually exists, inferences about the heredity of racial psychological traits would still be unwarranted. It has long been popularly believed that there are racial differences in such sensory processes as acuity of vision and hearing. The "primitive" man, such as the American Indian, was supposed to be superior to the "civilized" man in simple sensory performance (this superiority was in itself taken as a sign of inferiority, that is of a preintellectual stage of evolution).* The stereotype that the black man is a "born athlete" (as opposed to a "born" scientist or statesman) derives from this tradition. In this calculus, the cultural factors that mold behavior are ignored. Modern science on the whole has seen no evidence to refute the finding of the psychologist Woodworth who concluded over half a century ago, after studies of international subjects at the St. Louis Fair in 1904, that "On the whole, the keenness of the senses seems to be about on a par in the various races of mankind."

The few concrete findings of interracial genetic differences do not involve psychological characteristics. Rather, they concern such attributes as the ability to taste phenylthiocarbamide (PTC) and related compounds. There are also such well known biological findings as the higher incidence of sickle cell trait among blacks than among whites. Some investigators have suggested that there are differences in color perception related to distribution of hereditary color blindness among different populations. But the behavioral significance of such findings is obscure, if it exists at all.

For genetic racial differences in complex psychological attributes there is no evidence at all. "For the areas of human behavior that are vital in everyday life, for the varieties of behavior that allow individuals to participate satisfactorily in their society, there is no comparable evidence for genetically determined differences," concludes a comprehensive review of

---

* Thus a contributor the *Psychological Review* in 1895 compared the speed of sensory perception in a group of 12 whites, 11 Indians, and 11 blacks. When the white subjects proved to have the slowest reactions, this was taken as proof that they were the superior group. "Their reactions were slower because they belonged to a more deliberate and reflective race than did the members of the other two groups" (Gosset, p. 364).

the behavior-genetics literature (Spuhler and Lindzey, 1967).
A noted anthropologist (Fried, 1968) makes the same point:
"Absolutely no study yet done on a so-called racial sample of
human population adequately links intelligence, potential ability, educability or even achievement to a specific set of genetic
coordinates associated with any aggregate larger than a family
line or perhaps lineage."

3

It is not surprising, therefore, that leading geneticists, psychologists, and other scientists were startled by the appearance
in the *Harvard Educational Review* of Dr. Arthur R. Jensen's
widely publicized paper on race and IQ (Jensen, 1969). In
this article, Dr. Jensen, a professor of educational psychology
at the University of California at Berkeley, asserted that the
published studies justified the hypothesis that "genetic factors
are strongly implicated" in the average group differences between blacks and whites found on intelligence testing.

This position, in itself, was hardly a novel one. It had been
advanced for years by such strenuous critics of "the equalitarian dogma" as Henry E. Garrett, former head of Columbia
University's psychology department. Arguing that "The weight
of the evidence favors the proposition that racial differences
in mental ability (and perhaps in personality and character)
are innate and genetic," Garrett claimed that the scientific
community had been blinded to the truth by the duplicity of
Franz Boas, Communists, Jews, and sentimentalists (Garrett,
1961). Other racist psychologizers who found differences in
the native capacity of blacks and whites were Frank McGurk
(1956) and Audrey M. Shuey (1958). Their work formed the
"scientific" evidence for the diatribes of Wesley C. George,
Professor-Emeritus of Anatomy at the University of North
Carolina, who headed the white-supremacist North Carolina
Patriots, Inc., and Carleton Putnam, the Yankee businessman,
whose *Race and Reason* (1961) became a handbook of the
White Citizens' Councils.

Jensen's article is worth examining in some detail because it represents perhaps the most sophisticated presentation of the perennial contention that blacks are genetically inferior. Written by an influential educator and published in a prestigious journal, the article won headlines in the mass-circulation media. The entire 123-page article was reprinted in the *Congressional Record;* it was introduced as evidence by Southern schoolboards involved in desegregation suits; it formed a basis of White House policy discussions.*

Jensen reviews the psychological and educational literature indicating that blacks as a group score lower than whites on standard IQ tests. He concludes that the difference cannot be explained only by environmental factors such as poverty, discrimination, poor nutrition, and inferior schooling. Rather, he insists that genetic factors must also be "implicated." The average racial difference in inborn intelligence, Jensen further asserts, is not only quantitative in terms of IQ scores, but also qualitative. That is, he hypothesizes two genetically distinct intellectual processes which he labels Level I (associative ability) and Level II (conceptual ability). Jensen says that Level I, which is more proficient for rote learning and simple memory, is typically found among blacks, while Level II, which is more proficient for creative thinking and problem-solving, is characteristic for whites. In Jensen's view, attempts to provide compensatory education for disadvantaged children have "failed" because they were based on the assumption that blacks could attain the same level and quality of intelligence as whites.

The clear implication of this view is that educational goals for blacks should be more limited than for whites. In further exploring the implications of his position, Jensen expresses concern that "dysgenic trends" may be at work to "widen the genetic aspect of the average difference in ability between the Negro and white populations in the United States." Specifi-

---

* *Life* (June 12, 1970)

cally, he warns of the "danger that current welfare policies, unaided by eugenic foresight, could lead to the genetic enslavement" of black Americans.

Jensen's thesis has been reviewed carefully and exhaustively by leading authorities in many fields. With virtual unanimity they have found that the conclusions he draws from the studies he cites are unjustified, that his methodology and statistical analyses are faulty, and that even his summaries of a number of studies are inaccurate.* These critiques of Jensen are so extensive and cover so many separate issues that we cannot attempt to summarize them in this presentation.

For our present purpose, it is germane to highlight certain general implications in Jensen's approach to race.

4

To begin with, the issue of a hereditary factor in individual intelligence must not be confused with the question of racial differences. Much of Jensen's discussion is devoted to presenting evidence for a hereditary component in intelligence (for example, studies of twins raised in different environments). But even if, for the sake of argument, one accepts the validity of this evidence in individual families, this in no way supports an assertion that there is a comparable genetic difference be-

---

* For example, the man whom Jensen himself calls "our most eminent educational psychologist," Professor Lee J. Cronbach of Stanford University, writes: "I have detected substantial distortions in Jensen's report of some research and I must therefore warn the reader against accepting his summaries" (Cronbach, 1969). And another scholar who co-edited a volume with Jensen in 1968, Professor Martin Deutsch of New York University, reinforces Cronbach's charge and adds that all the erroneous statements, selective omissions, and arbitrary interpretations of the literature "are in the same direction: maximizing differences between blacks and whites and maximizing the possibility that such differences are attributable to hereditary factors." Deutsch (1969) observes that one of his colleagues came across 17 such errors in a casual perusal of Jensen's article. A number of authorities whose work was cited by Jensen to advance his argument have taken strong issue with his conclusions, and flaws in his use of heritability data have been noted by a number of experts. Thus, the appearance of careful scholarship is deceptive.

tween races. The leap from individual to racial genetics is unjustified by any existing evidence, as has already been noted. Jensen may be right in criticizing the "ostrich-like denial of biological factors in individual differences," but it is demagogic to imply that it is also ostrich-like to query the contention that there are genetic *racial* differences in intelligence. Jensen appeals to a common confusion. Racist thought often wraps itself in the banner of individual differences, while smothering such differences in group generalizations.

This position is typified by British psychologist H. J. Eysenck, who has taken up the cudgels for Jensen. Eysenck (1971) charges that Jensen's critics deny the inheritance of individual differences and are guilty of believing in the "innate equality" of all human beings, a creed that flies in the face of present-day knowledge. Eysenck is setting up a straw man. The principle that all men are created equal does not imply that they are all born alike. Equality is a concept of human rights, not of human ability, physiology, or temperament. Indeed, the concept of equality would not be very meaningful if individual and group differences did not exist. What the concept does insist upon is that persons of diverse genetic makeup should have unrestricted opportunity to develop the full repertoire of their capacities.

This is not only an ethical principle, but also a scientific judgment. For the denial of equal opportunity "stultifies the genetic diversity with which mankind became equipped in the course of its evolutionary development," as the noted geneticist Dobzhansky points out in his *Mankind Evolving* (1962). "Inequality conceals and stifles some people's abilities and disguises the lack of abilities in others. Conversely, equality permits (or rather, may permit, since a complete equality of opportunity has never existed except on paper) an optimal utilization of the wealth of the gene pool of the human species."

On a larger scale, this approach to individual differences applies to race differences. Such differences as may be demonstrable (and they have, of course, been distorted and exag-

gerated) have largely been interpreted as evidences of inequality; that is, of "superior" and "inferior" races. In recoil-
ing against this view, advocates of equality have sometimes
appeared to deny the existence of any differences whatsoever.
"The decisive point," says Dobzhansky, "is that nobody can
discover the cultural capacities of human individuals, populations, or races until they have been given something like an
equality of opportunity to demonstrate these capacities."
Educability is not concentrated in any one caste, class, or
race. "It does not follow, however, that to demonstrate 'equal'
capacities for cultural achievement all races will have to re-
produce copies of the civilizations and politics regarded as
quintessences of enlightenment and discernment in Washington or Moscow."

5

Jensen's use of the intelligence test to support his genetic
argument follows a tradition that goes back to the beginning
of the century. In 1905, the first of a series of intelligence
tests was introduced in France by Alfred Binet and Theodore
Simon. Their tests were designed for the practical and humanitarian purpose of screening feebleminded children so that they
should not be forced to compete with normal children in the
French school system. Binet and Simon were aware that scores
on their tests would be affected by environment and educational
opportunity. In setting up norms, they took it for granted
that the children they tested would come from closely similar
environments. But in the transatlantic migration, the tests
acquired an additional use—as a major instrument of "scientific racism." Administered with apparent evenhandedness to
white middle-class children and to black children brought up
under poverty and oppression, the tests were used not to
indict the racism that produced the unequal conditions and dis-
parate scores, but to confirm the racist insistence that blacks
are born less intelligent.

Leading the racist IQ movement was Lewis Terman of

Stanford University, one of the most eminent psychologists of his time, who adapted the Binet to American circumstances. In his influential book, *The Measurement of Intelligence,* published in 1916, the Stanford psychologist claimed his tests proved that a low level of intelligence was "very, very common among Spanish-Indian and Mexican families of the Southwest and also among Negroes. Their dullness seems to be racial . . ." (Terman, 1916). Terman asserted that the children of such persons "are uneducable beyond the merest rudiments of training. No amount of school instruction will ever make them intelligent voters or capable citizens in the true sense of the word. Judged psychologically they cannot be considered normal." This pronouncement of eternal doom neatly absolved the dominant white society and its schools from all responsibility and effort.

Group intelligence tests were first used on a mass scale during World War I, when military psychologists developed the Army Alpha and Army Beta tests for classifying nearly two million men. The Alpha was designed for general testing; the Beta was a non-language scale given to illiterates and foreign-born recruits with no command of English. These tests played a big part in making Americans "IQ-conscious" in the postwar years. "That the tests were still crude instruments was often forgotten in the rush of gathering scores and drawing practical conclusions therefrom," notes an authority on testing (Anastasi, 1968).

One of the main conclusions drawn from the Army data was that immigrants and Negroes were mentally inferior to the native white population. The lesson was plainly set forth by Dr. Robert M. Yerkes (1921), chief of the psychology division in the Surgeon General's Office. The tests, he asserted, "brought into clear relief . . . the intellectual inferiority of the negro. Quite apart from educational status, which is utterly unsatisfactory, the negro soldier is of relatively low grade intelligence." This finding, he added, "suggests that education alone will not place the negro race on a par with its Caucasian competitors." Dr. Yerkes also emphasized the inferiority of recent immigrant groups, and used the test data as arguments for rigid immigration quotas.

This thesis was echoed by a Princeton psychologist, Dr. Carl C. Brigham, in his widely quoted book *A Study of American Intelligence* (1923). In an enthusiastic foreword, Dr. Yerkes praised Dr. Brigham for confirming "the trustworthiness and scientific value of the statistical methods used by military psychologists." According to Brigham, the Army tests proved the superiority of the "Nordic type" over the Alpine, Mediterranean, and Negro groups. "Our figures," he also noted, "would rather tend to disprove the popular belief that the Jew is highly intelligent." Brigham predicted that as racial admixture increases, "American intelligence" would decline at an accelerating rate "owing to the presence here of the negro. These are the plain, if somewhat ugly, facts that our study shows."

That sounds rather conclusively factual, if somewhat ugly, and one can hardly blame Dr. Yerkes for greeting the Brigham study. But if that were the end of the story, this bit of history might not be worth recalling here. Seven years later, however, Brigham reviewed his studies in the *Psychological Review* and with admirable forthrightness repudiated his own work as unsound (Brigham, 1930). His concluding statement is a classic of self-criticism: "This review has summarized some of the more recent test findings which show that comparative studies of various national and racial groups may not be made with existing tests, and which show, in particular, that one of the most pretentious of these comparative racial studies—the writer's own—was without foundation." Brigham's candor is altogether commendable, but as Klineberg (1954) noted, "It is unfortunate that so many people have been influenced by the original study, whereas relatively few know the recantation."

While the Army tests provided ammunition for racists, they also contributed data that proponents of white superiority preferred to ignore. Black troops showed marked differences among themselves, and in many instances their scores were higher than those of whites. Thus blacks from the North scored much higher than those from the South. Moreover, blacks from several Northern states were superior to whites from a number of Southern states, if one were to judge by test results. As Benedict and Weltfish noted in *The Races of Mankind* (1943): "The white race did badly where economic conditions were bad and schooling was not provided, and Negroes living under better conditions surpassed them. The differences did not arise because people were from the North or the South, or because they were white or black, but because of differences in income, education, cultural advantages, and other opportunities." (Ironically, when these data from World War I were recalled during World War II in the pamphlet by Benedict and Weltfish, a number of Southern congressmen waxed indignant. The House Military Affairs Committee, under the chairmanship of Andrew J. May of Kentucky, conducted a secret investigation of Army plans to distribute this pamphlet.)

6

But the real issue, in any case, is not whether there are differences in the average test scores among various ethnic or class groups. It is the meaning of these differences that requires careful analysis. In general, the question of intelligence has been reduced to a kind of numbers game. The IQ number has exercised tyrannical sway in American education. In our zeal to measure and weigh, we tend to reduce the complex and intangible quality of "intelligence" to a readily "quantifiable" entity. All too often, the educator, psychologist, and social worker, when presented with an IQ number, have an imprecise understanding of its meaning and limitations.

The IQ reflects what an individual has learned, which is then wrongly presumed to indicate what he is inherently capable of learning. The IQ test measures an end product, not a potential. Even as a measure of achievement, however, the

IQ test is limited, since it measures only certain kinds of achievement and overlooks others. Moreover, the test may not register an individual's optimal response, since he may get a score that is lower than the one he might get if the test were given under different conditions. The results may be influenced by a number of emotional and motivational factors, such as the intrinsic interest of the test content, rapport with the examiner, intensity of the urge to compete with others, and past habits of solving problems. Many studies have directed attention to the effect of the examiner and the examining situation (Thomas *et al.*, 1971).

But even if the optimal score is obtained, one cannot assume that this is a measure of intrinsic ability. Before accepting the IQ number as a valid indication of intellectual potential, one must weigh many factors, including especially the effects of malnutrition and poor health.

The IQ can be useful as a prediction of school achievement if the children tested have a common social background and comparable school experience. But it cannot properly be used to make administrative judgments on children whose life experience differs radically from that of the white middle-class norm.

As a leading investigator of intelligence, J. P. Guilford, observes: "In comparing two racial groups on the basis of scores from a particular test, it would be important to know that the test measures the same ability or abilities in both groups. If it does not, the use of the scores would be like comparing weight for one group with basal metabolic rate for another" (Guilford, 1967). And Guilford concludes: "Sound deductions regarding racial differences are virtually impossible to infer from tests as now constituted. The search for culture-free or completely culture-fair tests is a futile and misleading objective."

Efforts to devise nonverbal "culture-free" tests have proved fruitless. Initial claims of success were honestly repudiated by Florence L. Goodenough after a review of studies pertaining to her Draw-a-Man Test. In 1926 she had reported racial differences, but by 1950 she had become convinced that "the search for a culture-free test, whether of intelligence, artistic ability, personal-social characteristics, or any other measurable trait is illusory, and that the naive assumption that the mere freedom from verbal requirements renders a test equally suitable for all groups is no longer tenable" (Goodenough and Harris, 1950). Goodenough now declared that her earlier report on ethnic differences in intelligence "is certainly no exception to the rule. The writer hereby apologizes for it."

The same criticism of "culture-free" tests is made by another authority, Anne Anastasi (1968), who notes that "Since every test measures a sample of behavior, it will reflect any factor that influences behavior. Persons do not react in a cultural vacuum." Any intelligence test favors individuals from the particular culture in which it was developed. For each culture encourages certain abilities and ways of behaving, discourages others. Persons do well or poorly on certain kinds of tests depending on their specific background. No test developed within a single cultural framework can serve as a universal yardstick for measuring "intelligence."

Jensen acknowledges that we have no answer to the question of what intelligence really is, but he nevertheless insists that we can measure it with precision. He never furnishes a clue to solve the mystery of measuring something without knowing what it is we are measuring. He simply repeats the traditional tautology that "intelligence is what the intelligence tests measure."

But assuming that the tests do accurately measure differences, on what basis can we conclude that these differences are predominantly due to heredity (80% in the white group, Jensen suggests) rather than environment? A leading geneticist, James F. Crow of the University of Wisconsin, notes that "a high heritability of intelligence in the white population would not, even if there were similar evidence in the black population, tell us that the differences between the groups are genetic.

No matter how high the heritability (unless it is 1), there is no assurance that a sufficiently great environmental difference does not account for the difference in the two means, especially when one considers that the environmental factors may differ qualitatively in the two groups. The failure, thus far, to find identifiable variables that, when matched, will equalize the IQ scores does not prove that the mean difference is hereditary. It can be argued that being white or being black in our society changes one or more aspects of the environment so importantly as to account for the difference. For example, the argument that American Indians score higher than Negroes in IQ tests—despite being lower on certain socio-economic scales—can and will be dismissed on the same grounds: some environmental variable associated with being black is not included in the environmental rating" (Crow, 1969).

7

In support of his thesis, Jensen cites the "failure" of compensatory education programs, such as Head Start. These programs were designed to provide the disadvantaged preschool child with an enriched and stimulating intellectual experience. Quoting reports that such programs have not significantly raised the IQ of black children, Jensen sees this as further evidence that genetic racial factors are responsible for their poor performance.

The fatal flaw in Jensen's reasoning is the assumption that these compensatory programs represented adequate efforts to stimulate the intellectual development of underprivileged children. On the contrary, the programs were often hastily constructed and insufficiently funded and staffed. The children were exposed to the special schools for short periods of time, with little follow-up effort. As noted by Dr. Jerome Kagan, Professor of Developmental Psychology at Harvard, it is unreasonable to conclude that compensatory education has failed merely because a program set up on a crash basis did not quickly produce sustained increases in IQ scores. "It would be nonsense to assume that feeding animal protein to a seriously malnourished child for three days would lead to a permanent increase in his weight and height, if after 72 hours of steak and eggs he was sent back to his malnourished environment" (Kagan, 1969).

Moreover, the compensatory programs were never very clear as to just what was being compensated for and what techniques were appropriate for achieving the vaguely formulated goals (Gordon and Wilkerson, 1966). The point is stressed by Dr. Edmund Gordon, former research director of Head Start and now professor of education at Teachers College, Columbia. He writes: "Like ethnic integration in public schools, compensatory education has not failed, it has simply not been actually implemented and evaluated. To assert that disadvantaged children have not responded under this special treatment is like claiming that medication doesn't help when the proper medicine has been unavailable. Such an assertion is fallacious and deceptive. We shall not know whether compensatory education, or for that matter just good education, works until we design appropriate programs, allocate the money required for them, train the people to run them and insure that they are adequately implemented. Any casual observer of the educational scene knows that these steps have not been taken" (Gordon, 1969).

Jensen's inference that black children can derive only limited benefit from special educational efforts in their behalf obviously has policy implications. Why spend money for upgrading schools for black people if their learning capacity is restricted by nature? Such thinking provides a perfect rationalization for those public officials, teachers, and taxpayers who resist the demands of black parents for decent schooling for their children. Jensenism, as Dr. Gordon observes, has become another excuse for failure to educate.

In the same vein, Jensen's concept of two levels of learning in blacks and whites (rote-memory learning vs. creative-conceptual learning) also serves to deny the validity of black

demands for equal education. The unscientific character of
Jensen's learning theory has been examined by educators who
have pointed out that the Level I-Level II system is a gross
oversimplification and distortion (Cronbach, 1969). If taken
seriously, this arbitrary dichotomy would justify two separate
school systems, one for training blacks in mechanical skills,
and the other for educating whites in the humanities, sciences,
and professions. The assignment of "vocational training" for
blacks has, of course, long been a kind of reflex response
 among American educators confronting black students.* Jensenism would confer scientific credentials on this practice—
not to mention a humanitarian aura, since Jensen offers to
unburden blacks of those tasks of thought for which nature
has not prepared them.

8

A most frightening issue raised by Jensen is the ideology
of eugenics applied to black people. It is hard to believe
—so soon after the Nazi nightmare—that proposals are again
being advanced to restrict reproduction on a racial basis. Yet
this is clearly the implication of Jensen's concern about the
danger of a decline in "our national IQ" resulting from a
higher birthrate among blacks than whites. He raises the
specter of "dysgenic trends," which he links with "current
welfare policies, unaided by eugenic foresight." The same fear
has been expressed by physicist William Shockley, one of the
most persistent agitators on the subject of black genetic inferiority: "Can it be that our humanitarian welfare programs
have already selectively emphasized high and irresponsible

---

* An eminent forerunner of Jensen, psychologist-educator E. L.
Thorndike, who also believed that "roughly 80% of mental capacity"
was genetically preordained, advocated separate paths based on inborn
abilities. Postulating a "deficiency of mental growth" in the children
of "inferior races," he asserted that "race directly and indirectly
produces differences so great that government, business, marriage,
friendship, and almost every other feature of human instinctive and
civilized life have to take account of a man's race" (Gossett, 1963).

rates of reproduction to produce a socially relatively unadaptable human strain?" (Shockley, 1966).

The cry that blacks are too prolific (for their own good, Jensen generously adds) ominously echoes the complaints of earlier eugenicists that Jews, foreign-born, and the poor of all colors and creeds are over-fertile and threaten to swamp "the American type," as Theodore Roosevelt put it. The eugenics craze that swept the United States earlier in this century contributed to the pressure for restrictive immigration laws culminating in the 1924 National Origins Quota Law. Psychologists and psychiatrists were not unaffected by this movement. "Under the influence of eugenic thinking, the burgeoning mental health movement picked up the cry," notes a historian of nativist ideas (Higham, 1963). "Disturbed at the number of hereditary mental defectives supposedly pouring into the country, the psychiatrists who organized the National Committee for Mental Hygiene succeeded in adding to the immigration bill of 1914 an odd provision excluding 'constitutional psychopathic inferiority.' By that time many critics of immigration were echoing the pleas in scientific periodicals for a 'rational' policy 'based on a noble culture of racial purity.' " In addition, state after state adopted sterilization laws which were often used selectively against blacks. As a committee of the American Neurological Association reported in 1935, "Though the avowed purpose of sterilization invariably starts out by being a genetic one, it often ends up becoming a social one." The racist purposes that such "eugenic" selectiveness could serve were monstrously exemplified in Nazi Germany, where eugenics became state religion, and the government, to insure against "dysgenic trends," ordered people to keep pedigree books like those kept by animal breeders.

Jensen and his supporters have raised a loud cry about their freedom to investigate genetic racial differences in intelligence. They charge their critics with trying to suppress them for political reasons. This is a false issue. As the material in this chapter indicates, the criticism leveled by the scientific

community against Jensen has essentially dealt with the unscientific nature of his argumentation. It is wholly legitimate
to expect an investigator in this field to exercise special care
because of the ever-present danger that his unverified assertions and hypotheses can be exploited for racist purposes. This
is an extraordinarily complex area of study, with many variables operating that have not been defined, let alone subjected
to systematic analysis. Highly pertinent is the comment on
Jensen made by black psychiatrist James P. Comer, Associate
Dean of Yale Medical School. Dr. Comer (1970) emphasizes
that careful and responsible scholarship must be protected, but
"it is not responsible science to make assumptions about the
meaning of black and white differences when the 'scientist' does
not know the black experience or fully understand or take into
account the implications of the experiental differences. Few
researchers have made a systematic appraisal of the impact of
inequitable and traumatic social policy." And because of their
failure to do so, it might be added, they have contributed to the
perpetuation of such policy.

3

"The Mark of Oppression"

STUDIES OF THE BLACK PERSON usually focus on what is abnormal in his life. He is viewed as a package of problems. "When we pick up a social science book," notes black historian Benjamin Quarles (1967), "we look in the index under 'Negro'; it will read, 'see Slavery,' 'see Crime,' 'see Juvenile Delinquency,' perhaps 'see Commission on Civil Disorders'; perhaps see anything except Negro. So when we try to get a perspective on the Negro, we get a distorted perspective."

The distortion is ubiquitous in the social and behavioral sciences, as other black scholars have pointed out. The literature on black families in America displays a "selective focus on the negative aspects," says Dr. Andrew Billingsley of Howard University in his *Black Families in White America* (1968). And in a review of psychiatric studies, Dr. Alyce C. Gullattee (1969) of St. Elizabeths Hospital, Washington, D. C., finds that white authors have "failed to accept the fact that Negroes can see themselves in a positive light."

The textbook approach to black people as "cases" has produced a caricature of their lives. A Swedish anthropologist, after living among blacks in Washington, D. C., for two years, was forcibly struck by the discrepancy between what he had always read and what he actually saw. In the professional literature "the image of the ghetto dweller becomes one of failure and impotence. It tells us little about how he goes about

45

life from day to day, coping with the people around him and
with the problems in his mind" (Hannerz, 1969).

This lopsided emphasis on pathology, even when motivated
by sympathy, results in dehumanization. Seen narrowly as a
"victim," the black man appears in the learned journals as a
patient, a parolee, a petitioner for aid, rarely as a rounded
human being. Small wonder that the black community is fed
up with being "researched" by investigators who can see only
the deforming marks of oppression. As novelist Ralph Ellison
(1967) writes about white observers of life in Harlem:

"I don't deny that these sociological formulas are drawn
from life. But I do deny that they define the complexity of
Harlem. They only abstract it and reduce it to proportions
which the sociologists can manage. I simply don't recognize
Harlem in them. And I certainly don't recognize the people of
Harlem whom I know. Which is by no means to deny the
ruggedness of life there, nor the hardship, the poverty, the
sordidness, the filth. But there is something else in Harlem,
something subjective, willful, and complexly and compellingly
human. It is that 'something else' that challenges the sociologists who ignore it, and the society which would deny its existence. It is that 'something else' which makes for our strength,
which makes for our endurance and our promise."

Ellison's comment on sociologists may well be taken to
heart by psychiatrists and psychologists. One of the vocational
hazards of psychiatry is a preoccupation with pathology. This
is understandable, since the clinician deals with people whose
emotional problems are troubling them enough to require professional assistance. But the result may be a one-sided view
of people. A strong tendency develops to regard personality in
terms of deficits rather than assets, weaknesses instead of
strengths. Racist attitudes can intensify this trend. When a
white psychiatrist indulges in sweeping generalizations about
the Negro's "basic personality" as characterized by "self-
hatred" or "fascination with feces" or "undirected hostility,"

the preoccupation with abnormality takes on overtones that
are unmistakably racist, regardless of the intention.

But the error of overgeneralizing the crippling impact of
oppression is not corrected by underestimating the harmful
consequences. There can of course be no question that a background of poverty, hunger, disease, and poor schooling has an
adverse and sometimes disastrous effect. The psychological
hazards and penalties are real. The destructive character of
segregation was recognized by the U.S. Supreme Court in its
1954 school decision. An important contribution to this decision was made by social psychologists, notably Kenneth Clark,
who showed how racism damages children. The psychological
toll of second-class citizenship and a sense of powerlessness
in American society is undeniable.

Yet it is profoundly wrong to assume that black people
have been overwhelmed by the destructive influences of the
racist society. It is one thing to recognize the social handicaps
that impede the fulfillment of an individual's potential. It is
quite another thing to conclude that the handicap has "crippled" him. Thus the flurry of studies in the 1960's on "cultural
deprivation" served a useful purpose in calling attention to
the obstacles that face children growing up in impoverished
homes. But these studies too often took for granted that the
child was inevitably and permanently damaged by these conditions. (See Chapter 5.)

The simplistic approach to pathology in black people rests
in part on a fallacious view of the consequences of stress. Severe stress may indeed produce basic distortions of psychological functioning. Exposure to semistarvation, military combat,
concentration camps, or natural disasters may lead to immediate and possibly long-range emotional disturbance, though
"some of the present concepts regarding individual reaction
to stress are based on little, if any evidence" (Hocking, 1970).

But stress may also stimulate healthy coping mechanisms.
Reactions to stress are always highly individualized, depending on a multiplicity of factors such as pre-existing personality

characteristics, constitutional factors, and training. In different persons subjected to the same stress, the response may range from constructive adaptation to a breakdown of normal functioning. Rarely can one predict exactly how a given individual will react under circumstances of special stress. Some people unexpectedly marshal resources that were not previously visible, while others who seemed to be towers of strength collapse. Obviously, if the stress is sufficiently severe and protracted, it may finally have a very damaging effect on anyone.

Certain symptoms often develop as a result of stress. A degree of anxiety or depression is not uncommon. Rage reactions may occur. While such symptoms are undesirable and can produce great discomfort, they do not necessarily reflect a basically unhealthy personality. Moreover, unhealthy responses to stress may be remediable, given changes in life circumstances and in coping patterns.

To be sure, some psychological changes resulting from stress may be permanent. To pretend otherwise would be Pollyannish. But there is great variation in the degree and severity of symptoms. Some symptoms may coexist with healthy trends and be subordinate to them. In other cases, the disturbance becomes the dominant feature determining the individual's functioning.

2

Unfortunately, many authors ignore the individuality and range of reactions to stress. And this error is compounded in studies of blacks. An outstanding example is Kardiner and Ovesey's influential book, *The Mark of Oppression* (1951), which defines the black's "basic personality" in terms of the stigmata of his condition in America. The stress of racist discrimination has produced not merely an inerasable mark but a deformity in the black man's psyche. Using global terms, Kardiner and Ovesey conclude that "There is not one personality trait of the Negro the source of which cannot be traced to his difficult living conditions. There are no exceptions to this rule. The final result is a wretched internal life. . . ."

Closely linked to the concept that black people are universally overwhelmed by the stress of their condition in America is the thesis that they all suffer from low self-esteem. The major hypothesis of *The Mark of Oppression* is that "The Negro has no possible basis for a healthy self-esteem and every incentive for self-hatred."* The authors contend that while the Negro is not racially inferior in a genetic sense, discrimination has created in him a sense of inferiority. The "basic Negro personality" is a "caricature of the corresponding white personality, because the Negro must adapt to the same culture, must accept the same social goals, but without the ability to achieve them." Three traits in particular are characteristic: "the conviction of unlovability, the diminution of affectivity, and the uncontrolled hostility."

What disturbs the Negro most, in the authors' view, is that he must identify himself with Negroes. He therefore adopts a compensatory identification with the white man, whom he also hates. "The enormous amount of aggression that is mobilized in the Negro in itself prevents any healthy self-esteem from getting a foothold. Here, retaliatory fears and conscience mechanisms interfere." Middle-class blacks are particularly vulnerable to depressed self-esteem. "Their ideal formation is of a high order, but founders on the rock of unattainable (white) ideals. The fact that these ideals are relatively more capable of achievement than in the lower class renders the conflict sharper."

These sweeping generalizations are based on psychoanalytic interviews with 25 subjects. Eleven of the 25 were paid

---

* Some of the evidence of black self-hatred adduced by Kardiner and Ovesey seems remarkably farfetched. They observe that one of their patients "insists that she is not Negro, but Afro-American, indicating how deeply vulnerable she is on the subject of color. This means that her predominant trait is self-hatred. . . ." As one black reviewer was moved to wonder, "Could it be that Afro-American means white?" (Collins, 1952).

$1.50 per session (with a bonus at the end of the twentieth interview to induce the subjects to stay with the study). Twelve others received psychotherapy in return for relating their life stories. The remaining two subjects were volunteers. All but one of the 25 had symptoms of psychological disturbance. For this small and obviously unrepresentative sample, Kardiner and Ovesey set up the vaguest of all possible experimental controls. "Our constant control is the American White Man," they stated. "We require no other control."

The authors argued that from the standpoint of psychodynamic analysis 25 cases are a large number. "Let the reader recall that Freudian psychodynamics were set forth on the basis of five published cases." This may stimulate doubts about Freudian psychodynamics in the minds of some readers, but in any event the point is irrelevant. For these authors are not discussing psychodynamic processes in individuals; they are attempting a psychosocial analysis of a whole people. They are not bothered by the absence from their sample of blacks who function in a psychologically healthy way. On the contrary, they assume throughout that such persons, if they do exist, are deviations from the "basic Negro personality." It is always "the Negro" who "identifies himself with feces," is "vindictive and vituperative," and fails in his social relations with other black men because "in every Negro he encounters his own projected self-contempt." This psychodynamic inventory of Negro personality turns into a psychological chamber of horrors, "the consequence of many generations of being a slave."

The Mark of Oppression was sharply criticized by a number of black authors when the book was published in 1951.*

---

* A detailed critique by C. W. Collins (1952) in the *Journal of the National Medical Association* was followed in the same journal by a symposium of black physicians. See also the article by Lloyd L. Brown (1952). As these critical reviews indicate, the benefit of hindsight was not required to detect the injurious fallacies of the Kardiner-Ovesey thesis about the Negro's "wretched internal life." Yet the book has continued to exert enormous influence and is still ubiquitously

Essentially, these critics pointed out that in generalizing about black Americans Kardiner and Ovesey were blind to all that was strong and healthy in the life of blacks. The book described a crushed and crippled people. "Obviously," the psychiatrists asserted, "Negro self-esteem cannot be retrieved, nor Negro self-hatred destroyed, as long as the status is quo." But according to the "caricature of the corresponding white personality" drawn by Kardiner and Ovesey, the status would have to remain quo indefinitely. For there is no indication whatsoever in their book that black men and women could generate enough creative and collective force to change it. Within a few years, however, the course of history decisively refuted this image of a crushed people. The powerful thrust of the black liberation movement dramatically testified to the courage, determination, and resourcefulness of masses of blacks —qualities that could arise only from psychological health, not pathology. And these qualities were not produced by a change in the status quo; on the contrary, they forced such a change.

Incredibly, the authors saw no reason to change their thesis in the preface to a 1962 reissue of their book. "Our deepest satisfaction," they now wrote, "is derived from the fact that the American Negro, whom we found so crushed eleven years ago, today is a group alive, seeking and finding a more rewarding role in American society" (Kardiner and Ovesey, 1962).

But how could it happen that a people so "crushed" were able to come alive in one decade? No miracle had taken place.

---

cited as authoritative support for such generalizations about "the Negro personality." Even so astute an observer as Robert Coles (1967), whose findings refute the thesis, appears to believe that it can be balanced with contradictory data. "Though in no way do I deny what Kardiner and Ovesey have called 'the mark of oppression,' he writes, "it remains equally true that alongside suffering I have encountered a resilience and an incredible capacity for survival." Perhaps the positive characteristics that Coles discovered in black people would have come as less of a revelation had psychiatric education been free of dogmas about black pathology.

The black people had been crushed only by the generalizations
of the authors. Blacks were a "group alive" in 1951 as indeed
they had been in all the years of their history of struggle and
aspiration. What Kardiner and Ovesey were attesting to was
not the long slumber of the black psyche but their own ignorance of a long and unceasing fight for freedom and dignity,
now reaching new heights of determination.

3

It is of course true that a social system in which "white
is right" presents a serious threat to the self-esteem of black
Americans. They are bombarded with accusations of inferiority, spoken or unspoken, in classroom, employment office,
courthouse, and the media. As Kenneth Clark observes in
Dark Ghetto (1965), "Human beings who are forced to live
under ghetto conditions and whose daily experience tells them
that almost nowhere in society are they respected and granted
the ordinary dignity and courtesy accorded to others will, as a
matter of course, begin to doubt their own worth." But the
threat to self-esteem does not have uniform consequences.
Some individuals may be overwhelmed. Others become aware
of the source of the threat, develop appropriate anger at the
injustices they suffer, and focus their energies on the struggle
against oppression. Still others may show a mixture of healthy
and unhealthy responses which express themselves differently
in different situations. Conclusions drawn from individuals in
psychoanalytic treatment are bound to have a one-sided emphasis on the pathological, as a result of both the nature of
the sample and the pathology-oriented theory of psychoanalysis. Such conclusions, as is so evident in *The Mark of Oppression*, not only make the error of stereotypic over-general-
ization, but also fail to distinguish those expressions of
pathology that are remediable and incidental from those which
may be deep-seated and dominant.

The hazards of generalizing about the self-concept of
blacks are emphasized in a review of studies on the subject

which concludes that "The research findings can only be described as incomplete, fragmentary, and at times contradictory" (Proshansky and Newton, 1968). This is not surprising in view of the methodological confusions that mark this field of investigation. As the authors note, "Techniques for measuring self-concept have often seemed artificial; reports have frequently been highly subjective, and the number of subjects has been typically small." Other pitfalls have been noted by Simpson and Yinger (1965), who emphasize the great variability in the effects of prejudice on minority group members, depending on age, education, occupation, temperament, intergroup contact, group cohesiveness, and many other factors.

Findings on self-esteem may also depend on the historic period and social context of the study. In their classic investigations in the late 1930's, the Clarks found that black children tended to deprecate themselves when asked to choose between dark-skinned and white dolls in terms of "being bad" and "looking nice" (Clark and Clark, 1939). However, a study done in the late 1960's by Jeanne Spurlock (1969), chairman of the Department of Psychiatry at Meharry Medical College, found that in a group of black children aged 4 to 9, all showed definite awareness of racial differences as related to color, and none manifested negative feelings about their own color. "This situation has shifted since black has become beautiful," Dr. Spurlock observes. "Coloring books for the young child are geared to black identity; black dolls are flooding the market."

There is thus abundant psychological justification for the new emphasis on black pride. Teaching children that "black is beautiful" is a healthy corrective to the lesson long inculcated by white society that black is blemished.

Instead of self-derogation, anger may be the response to oppression. This is frequently characterized in the psychiatric literature as "hostility" or "rage." The difficulty with such terms is that they are often used as designations of pathology.

The term "anger" is more appropriate because it connotes the recoil of a healthy rather than a damaged or weak personality.

The black man's anger may not be overtly displayed to whites in situations where such expressions might be self-defeating. Then the black man is described as abnormally acquiescent. But when he does manifest his anger, he is likely to be accused of "blind rage," "running amok," "impulsive violence" and other symptoms of illness. A traditional feature of the racist syndrome is the interpretation of strength of feeling in the black man as primitive emotionalism. The affective reaction is more often seen as "excessive" than as "appropriate." But the anger of the oppressed man is a sign of health, not pathology. It says: "I am condemning you for doing wrong to me."

The concept of "Black Rage" has been elaborated by Grier and Cobbs (1969). These black psychiatrists write; "People bear all they can and, if required, bear even more. But if they are black in present-day America they have been asked to shoulder too much. They have had all they can stand. They will be harried no more. Turning from their tormentors, they are filled with rage." In order to survive, the black man has had to develop "cultural paranoia, in which every white man is a potential enemy unless he personally finds out differently." Allied with this cultural paranoia are "cultural depression," "cultural masochism," and "cultural antisocialism," all of which traits Grier and Cobbs feel are adaptive devices for " 'making it' in America, and clinicians who are interested in the psychological functioning of black people must get acquainted with this body of character traits which we call the Black Norm."

This thesis may be more accurate than that of Kardiner and Ovesey, but like theirs it is based on a selected sample of patients from which the authors too easily draw generalizations about all black people. In a review of the book, Hugh Butts (1969), senior psychiatrist at Harlem Hospital, noted that the conclusions of *Black Rage* are biased by the authors'

looking only at psychiatric patients who seek help because of
marked adaptive failure. Ignored, Butts maintains, are the
millions of blacks who are adapting with varying degrees of
success. From another viewpoint, the book has been criticized
in *The Black Scholar* (1970) for attempting to discover the
cause of group behavior by analyzing a few individuals. Grier
and Cobbs provide insight into the psychodynamic functioning
of their black patients, but they fall into over-simple formulations that distort the impact of racism.

The forward surge of the past ten years could not have
taken place if most black people were mired in the low self-
esteem and self-respect often attributed to them. Nor will it
do to explain this upsurge as a "reaction-formation" against
low self-esteem. That is another device for dissolving the
black man's strengths in the terminology of psychodynamics.*

Like Kardiner and Ovesey, other psychiatrists have had
to take note of the apparent discrepancy between the defeated
Negro depicted in their earlier studies and the militant black
who is pressing for radical changes in American life. For example, Kennedy (1952) concluded that the neuroses of blacks
appeared to be caused by "conflicts arising from a hostile,
white ego ideal. The self-hatred, generated by the fact of not
being white, started with earliest infancy." Ten years later,
Kennedy (1963) observed that the blacks had made "gigantic
strides in the direction of creating their own ego ideals" and she
asked that her 1952 paper be interpreted in the context of its

---

* Some authors, apparently baffled when they run across evidence
that contradicts the stereotype of black self-hatred, outflank the evidence with a psychodynamic interpretation. Thus a study of educational climates in high schools (McDill et al., 1966) asserts that "High
self-esteem on the part of Negroes is a defense mechanism against
discrimination." Here again, a psychological explanation is invoked
to explain away a positive manifestation in blacks as only another
expression of pathology. Presumably, if a black person is to pass the
test of normality he must manifest low self-esteem. For a detailed critical review of the literature on this subject, see McCarthy and Yancey
(1971). These sociologists conclude by questioning the theoretical
assumptions and purported evidence for the basic hypothesis that
blacks are "very likely" to manifest negative self-esteem.

composition "before the meaningful events of the intervening decade and the effect that this recent history has already had upon the changing Negro personality."

It is certainly a reasonable request that one's article be viewed in its proper historical context, and there is no doubt that the liberation movement of the 1950's and 1960's registered great advances in black self-awareness. But this movement has deep roots in history. What Kardiner and Kennedy seem to be suggesting is that only blacks have changed and their own views require no revision. It is incumbent on all of us to reconsider previous generalizations in the light of new perspectives gained in the past two decades. The struggles of black people today should open our eyes to dimensions of personality that may have escaped our notice in the past. Otherwise one has to view the "new Negro" as a phoenix arising out of the ashes rather than as the embodiment, on a higher level, of healthy strivings that were never smothered, despite all the efforts of an oppressive society. The social blows may bruise, but they do not necessarily crush.

4

The Illusion of Color
Blindness

THE TENDENCY TO VIEW all blacks as permanently scarred by
their racist environment coexists with an apparently opposite
tendency to minimize or deny the impact of oppression. The
first approach, as noted in the preceding chapter, views the
black man's social existence as inescapably pathogenic.
"There has never been a Negro born in America who has not
been crippled and maimed by the great lie of racial inferiority," asserts C. Eric Lincoln in *My Face Is Black* (1964).
In contrast, other authors seem to regard the black man's special experience in America as a secondary phenomenon, perhaps determining the form of his behavior but not its essential
content. In this perspective, the black becomes "a white man
in a black skin." The impact of racism on personality is considered superficial and subordinate to psychodynamic forces
that are presumed to be universal.

The two approaches appear to start from opposite positions but in reality are committed to the same postulate—
black people are to be understood in terms of intrapsychic
pathology. In the first case, blacks are seen as disfigured vic-
tims of the oppressive society. In the second, the failure to
grasp the social context of behavior results in interpreting behavior as deviant even when it is realistic and normally adap-

tive. The black man's justified suspicion of white people is mistakenly identified as paranoia pure and simple. His bitter protest against a boss or slumlord is seen as an expression of "Oedipal hostility."

As a concession to the growing awareness of social and cultural influences on behavior, some psychiatrists now acknowledge that these may act as "triggering mechanisms." According to this concept, racism touches off psychodynamic processes that then unfold in classical patterns. Such a view has little in common with an interactionist approach that sees environmental issues as being involved in a basic way, on all levels, from the beginning of personality development.

"Color-blindness" is no virtue if it means denial of differences in the experience, culture, and psychology of black Americans and other Americans. These differences are not genetic, nor do they represent a hierarchy of "superior" and "inferior" qualities. But to ignore the formative influence of substantial differences in history and social existence is a monumental error.

It is therefore noteworthy that the leading contemporary textbooks in psychiatry either overlook completely or give only a glancing reference to the blacks and their special problems in American society. The 7th edition of the Kolb-Noyes *Modern Clinical Psychiatry* (1968) contains no reference in its index to Negro, black, race, or racism. Neither does Freedman and Kaplan's *Comprehensive Textbook of Psychiatry* (1967), even though many of its contributors have a stronger social emphasis than is evident in the other volume. Only marginal reference is made in Lidz (1968) and in Redlich and Freedman (1966). Standard histories of psychiatry, such as those by Zilboorg (1941) and Alexander and Selesnick (1966), ignore the subject.

The notion that blacks lack any characteristics of a distinct culture—that they are Americans and nothing else—has become "almost a dogma of liberal social science" (Blauner, 1970). The black man was described by Myrdal (1944) as "an exaggerated American" whose culture is merely "a distorted development, or a pathologic condition" of American culture in general. Glazer and Moynihan (1963) maintain that "The Negro is only an American, and nothing else. He has no values and culture to guard and protect." And a psychiatrist who has written extensively about black patients, Dr. E. B. Brody of the University of Maryland, asserts that the Negro "has, technically speaking, no culture of his own" (Brody, 1966).

Such observations suggest the great distance from which black people are generally viewed by white authors. The unique history of the black people in America simply disappears in these formulations. "To say that a people have no culture is to say that they have no common history which has shaped and taught them. And to deny the history of a people is to deny their humanity," comments Billingsley (1968). The black experience has of course, not been uniform; it has varied according to time and place; and its consequences have been diverse and complex. But to deny that a common body of experience has shaped a black culture is to shut off the possibility of understanding black psychology.

The blindness to black cultural patterns and values is due, in part, to the mistaken notion that there are universal personality trends which can be understood in isolation from a specific social setting. It is widely assumed, for example, that "Oedipal conflicts" are common to all cultures and therefore provide a master key to all motivational systems. Yet Malinowski discovered that this presumably universal phenomenon did not occur among the Trobriand Islanders, and Frantz Fanon noted that it was virtually non-existent in Martinique. A growing body of evidence has demonstrated that there is a dynamic interaction between the human organism and its culture, and that it is impossible to abstract an individual's lifestyle from the culture that helps to mold it and through which it is expressed.

While this concept has long been understood by anthropologists and social psychologists, it has had less influence on the thinking and practice of clinical psychiatrists. In both the diagnosis and treatment of disturbed personalities, the interactionist approach has been applied only sporadically. More characteristic have been the attempts to fit the black experience into a rigid Freudian formula. The black man becomes an illustration of a universal instinctual pattern.

2

Freudian theory has even been used to explain black history in terms of the stages of individual development charted by this theory: oral, anal, phallic, and prepubertal. In this schema, the initial phase of development is the oral stage, in which the infant is wholly dependent on a provider. Applying this concept to black Americans, Sharpley (1969) suggests that slavery took mature men and women and thrust them into a system that caused regression to the oral stage. Now (at long last) the Negro is reaching for maturity, and an analogy is drawn between "the tasks that confront the Negro as a people and confront children in their psychosexual growth."

Such analogies always limp, but this one seems singularly lame. Even if one were to agree with the conventional description of psychodynamic stages, the comparison with the development of a whole people can only confuse matters and buttress the stereotype of the "childlike" black. It is simply not true that the economic dependency of the slave made him an infant in either thought or feeling. Sharpley says, "What I have not mentioned is his feeling throughout these phases"—a not insignificant omission.

This approach is also illustrated in a discussion of the black's intrapsychic structure, past and present, by Hunter and Babcock (1967). These psychiatrists point out that forcible transplantation of the African into an alien culture must have profoundly affected his emotional life. They then theorize that the black man was reduced to infantile dependency, but without gratification of his infantile needs for love and conditions necessary for maturation. The plantation owner was a parental surrogate. The relationship served the narcissism and possessiveness of the master. A pathologic "symbiosis" existed between him and his slave, analogous to the unhealthy tie between infant and parent postulated by Margaret Mahler in her studies of the genesis of psychosis in children. This relationship, say Hunter and Babcock, is "reminiscent of the need of some women who, undifferentiated from their own mothers, become pregnant in order to consolidate their unconscious, often phallic, narcissistic position by extending themselves through a renewal of their earlier symbiotic dependency. The infant conceived out of such motives will be psychologically vulnerable to those aberrations involved in the maturing process. Such aberrations arise from the direct expressions of the conscious and unconscious conflicts and strivings in the parents, from the ego-defensive operations against the conflicts, and from the parental reactions when the infants not only fail to resolve the parents' conflicts but rather augment them."

In this view, the black under slavery could not develop the capacity to function independently. With emancipation, he reached the "separation-individuation" phase of the young child, but his handicap was too great. "In view of his unprepared ego," continue Hunter and Babcock, "the permission to individuate, given by law to the Negro slave in 1863, was essentially a useless privilege. Clinical material of psychoanalysis is replete with evidence of failure in ego development in individuals who, because of regression or of fixation, have remained unconsciously tied—that is, indifferentiated—from the objects of their early childhood." The authors further speculate that the black man felt caught in the rivalries between North and South "as do some children who are made the battleground on which the two parents fight out their conscious and unconscious conflicts. Psychoanalytic studies of such cases have demonstrated that the children are, in essence,

emotionally rejected by both parents and grow to chronologi-
cal adulthood with ego impairment that reflects the specific
dynamics of each parent, specifically and in interaction."

This approach typifies a fairly extensive body of literature
in which the theoretical assumptions of psychoanalysis are
used to explain the black psyche in terms of deviant child development.* Psychoanalytic case studies serve as the model
for historical investigation of the black people. The appeal is
not to historical evidence but to a structure of psychodynamic
theory presented as clinical findings.**

Other psychoanalytic writings maintain that in certain of
the black man's demands on white people an unconscious
irrational component is mixed in with just claims for redress
of grievances. This view was advanced in a series of often-
quoted psychogenetic studies in race relations reported by
Helen V. McLean. The Negro's hostility against whites, the
psychiatrist maintained (McLean, 1946), "leads to anxiety
and guilt because he needs and is dependent on white men.
From this anxiety he wishes to escape by a passive submission.
He longs for an omnipotent perfect father whom he can trust
implicitly. . . . His own masculine pride will not allow him to
admit these unmasculine longings, so his angry protest mounts.
One source for the anger is the real discrimination. This is
used to rationalize his need to protest against his more passive
self. The greater the protest, the greater the anxiety and the
unconscious wish to give up the whole struggle." Like most
psychodynamic descriptions of blacks, this one is unrestrained
in its generalizations, a torrent of typology.

Also characteristic of psychoanalytic explanations is the

---

* It is sad to note that the crude analogies between blacks and
children drawn over half a century ago in the early psychoanalytic
literature (see Chapter 1) are still presented as self-evident truths.

** As noted in the previous chapter, Kardiner and Ovesey in *The
Mark of Oppression* base their elaborate conceptualizations of black
personality on a skimpy and unrepresentative sample of 25 subjects
(11 paid). Hunter and Babcock do even better. Their total sample
consisted of one patient.

misevaluation of the objective cause of black anger—the real oppression. This is seen not as the main feature of the individual's situation but simply as an instrument for rationalizing an emotional need. The black man does not want to struggle; he wants to submit. His militancy is a facade. Such explanations of the black man's rebellion reduce it to a mere posture. And the longing for an "omnipotent perfect father whom he can trust implicitly" would appear to echo the creaky stereotype of the "childlike Negro."

McLean also has a psychoanalytic explanation for the charge of "Uncle Tom" leveled against black leaders who are doing "really constructive work." She considers this a "typical sour grapes reaction" stemming from unconscious envy of their acceptance by white men. According to this interpretation, black leaders become "like brothers and sisters fighting for the preferred position with the mother or father." Again the black man's anger is stripped of its genuineness and validity. The psychoanalytic reductionism unerringly finds the core of pathology which it habitually seeks.

3

In order to judge what is healthy or morbid in an individual's psychological functioning, one must be aware of what is appropriate and effective behavior within his specific cultural milieu. If this principle is not kept in mind, the psychiatrist can easily fall into the error of using his own social, economic, or cultural status and values as the norm. Differences in the patient's position then represent pathological deviations. Often overlooked is the fact that the same overt behavior patterns may mean very different things to people from different cultural backgrounds. What may be interpreted as pathology in one situation may actually represent a healthy adaptation in another (Chess, Clark, and Thomas, 1953).

Yet psychiatric clinics tend to shy away from inquiries into the cultural background of patients. As Karno (1966) points out, "Because the psychiatric history interview derives

from the model of the traditional medical history, it tends to
exclude socio-cultural factors when they may be important
to diagnosis and treatment." Thus, one therapist at the California Neuropsychiatric Institute failed to record a single fact
about the ethnicity of his patients (many of whom were blacks
and Mexican-Americans), their language, or family relationships, despite an otherwise detailed evaluation in the tradition
of the medical-psychiatric history. As a result of such insensi-
tivity, many patients simply do not show up after a few weeks.
Karno suggests that "There may be a conscious or unconscious
avoidance of the reality of ethnicity stemming from a hypersensitive concern not to be 'discriminating' or 'prejudiced' in
the clinic setting." This may be a factor, but more likely the
avoidance reflects a simple lack of understanding and concern.
In any case, it is the patient who suffers.

Unfortunately, most psychiatric textbooks are of little help
in this regard, as we have noted. And the criteria for psychiatric diagnosis and classification are too often taught in an
abstract, generalized fashion that omits cultural considerations. The student is not alerted to the limitations of his own
cultural perspective. Ethnocentric attitudes are bound to result
in a prejudicial approach to the black patient.

This has been documented in many studies. It has been
noted that in a psychiatric emergency room, the diagnosis and
disposition of the patient vary with race. A study by Gross
and others (1969) dealt with 2,279 patients who visited the
daytime service of the Psychiatric Institute of the University
of Maryland School of Medicine. The investigators found that
behavior requiring hospitalization of a female patient was
more often perceived as neurotic when the patient was white,
and as schizophrenic when the patient was black. This variation is attributed to the clinician's response set. He is pre-
disposed to base such decisions on his own social and cultural
experiences. In dealing with a white patient, the white resident
tends to give a more empathic diagnosis—for example, neurotic reaction—and to make a more optimistic disposition.

With a black patient, he overreacts to some behaviors, pays too little attention to others. He is a prisoner of his ethnocentric attitudes, though he would no doubt be shocked to be told that he is less than objective.

Differences in frames of reference are largely unrecognized by psychological theorists who uncritically accept the premises of the dominant culture. Even black psychologists, it has been argued, "are still operating with a lot of assumptions and machinery that have been developed by white psychologists primarily for white people" (White, 1960). What appear to be contradictions in black behavior, for example, may be due to the fact that their social experience has given them a greater tolerance of ambiguity, suggests Dr. Joseph White, Director of Black Studies at the University of California at Irvine.

Dr. White also cites differences in the psychology of culture heroes. The white hero of tradition is "infallible and rigid, scores his triumphs with inhuman skill and retires undefeated. In the black culture, the hero is by and large the brother who messes with the system and gets away with it." Being "color-blind"—that is, oblivious to the specific features of black culture—the conventional psychological models misinterpret strengths as deficits. "Many children growing up in the black community learn a certain kind of mental toughness. They learn survival skills. They know how to jive the school principal, and they show a lot of psychological cleverness and originality in the particular style they emerge with. They know how to deal with the credit man; they know how to deal with the cat at the corner market; they know how to deal with hypes and pimps. But most institutions have not yet learned how to appreciate and capitalize upon this particular kind of style" (White, 1970).

As Dr. White reminds us, "One of the very different kinds of things about the black culture and the black psyche of America is that it is an oral culture—the blues, the gospel songs, the heavy rap, the sermon and traditions are carried orally, and people are going to have to examine that oral ex-

pression in order to make new insights into the psychological
functioning of black people. . . . We must develop a kind of
psychological jiu-jitsu and recognize that what the dominant
culture deems deviant or anti-social behavior might indeed
be the functioning of a healthy black psyche which objectively
recognizes the antagonisms of the white culture and develops
machinery for coping with them."

Obviously, the need to know the specific cultural context
to fully explain the symptom does not mean that illness, where
it really exists, is thereby explained away. The fact that many
blacks are misdiagnosed as paranoid, when their suspicious-
ness may be justified by their life experiences, does not mean
that a black person cannot suffer from paranoid schizophrenia
or other illnesses with paranoid features. A black's intense
anger may represent a healthy reaction to racist indignity, but
in some cases it may reflect hostility based on irrational
psychoneurotic disturbances.

The pychiatrist does the black a great disservice when he
ignores the socio-cultural parameters that may be determining
the patient's behavior. But it is no service to explain away
all deviant behavior as a normal and justified reaction to an
oppressive environment. This, on the white psychiatrist's part,
would simply be another form of patronizing that would de-
prive a black patient of necessary therapy. Genuine respect
for the black means approaching him truly as an individual
human being and without preconceived stereotypes. But as
with any other human being, what he is as an individual involves his specific social experiences. The white psychiatrist
who likes to think he is "color blind" may be as far off the
mark as the psychiatrist who is blinded by color.

5

The Deficient "Deficit" Model

IN THE CURRENT JARGON of the social sciences, the poor are
frequently identified by various euphemisms such as "disadvantaged," "underprivileged," and "socially handicapped."*
Perhaps the most sweeping of these labels is the designation
of poor people as "culturally deprived." So tenacious is this
term that psychologist Frank Riessman (1962), who wrote
a book questioning its appropriateness, decided to employ
The Culturally Deprived Child as his title "because it is the
term in current usage," thus giving further circulation to the
concept. During the 1960's, "culturally deprived" became a
code term for poor blacks.

The substitution of "culturally deprived" for "poor" is not
a simple shift in terminology for identical phenomena. It represents a significant shift in outlook. Traditionally, poverty was
measured primarily in terms of objective, concrete conditions
of life: income, housing, nutrition, medical care. The concept
of "cultural deprivation" places the emphasis on the psychological characteristics of the poor individual himself—his language use, perceptual level, cognitive style, emotional attributes. As one sociologist has observed, poverty nowadays is
often discussed as if it were a personal trait rather than a
social condition.

* Federal agencies have instructed their staffs to avoid the four-
letter word and use "low-income group" instead.

This shift has important consequences. It means a redirection of concern, from overcoming the objective circumstances of poverty to altering the attributes of people who are poor.

Originally, the notion of cultural deprivation arose in opposition to the postulate of inborn group inferiority. It was developed by psychologists and educators who sought to place on society the onus for school failure of poor black children and other minorities. The theorists of cultural deprivation hypothesized that poor children suffered from inadequate mental stimulation, both quantitatively and qualitatively, and that this resulted in a number of psychological deficits. Unlike the pseudo-geneticists, these theorists regarded such deficits as remediable if treated early enough in childhood. And they strove to compensate for the damage by enriched stimulation through preschool programs such as Head Start.

There is, of course, a certain plausibility to this approach. Otherwise it would not have been so influential among professionals of good will. The penalties of poverty are not illusory. A poor child is not likely to bring to his beginning school career the advantages that a middle-class child usually will—experience with the kind of books and toys that he will encounter in school, familiarity with the kind of language his teachers will use, contact with the larger world beyond his own neighborhood.

But these limitations have been viewed narrowly and patronizingly. Implicit in the concept of "cultural deprivation" has been the assumption that the standards of the dominant white middle-class culture represent norms by which all other cultures may be appropriately measured. Deviations from the ethnocentric norm are viewed as deprivations. "If your children don't have our kind of toys and talk our kind of language, they must be handicapped," the argument runs. It is taken for granted that cultural departures from the middle-class model mean cultural deficits. Instead of understanding differences in language or behavioral style as reflecting adaptations that may be appropriate to the child's environment, such differences are dogmatically rated according to their approximation of the middle-class model. The closer to this model, the smaller the deficit; the further from this model, the larger the deficit.

Kenneth Clark (1965) underscores this point in discussing what he calls "the cult of 'cultural inferiority.' " He writes: "Just as those who proposed the earlier racial inferiority theories were invariably members of the dominant racial groups who presumed themselves and their groups to be superior, those who at present propose the cultural deprivation theory are, in fact, members of the privileged group who inevitably associate their privileged status with their own innate intellect and its related educational success. Such association neither proves nor disproves the theory in itself, but the implicit caste and class factors in this controversy cannot and should not be ignored. Many of today's scholars and teachers came from 'culturally deprived' backgrounds. Many of these same individuals, however, when confronted with students whose present economic and social predicament is not unlike their own was, tend to react negatively to them. . . ."

2

In the past decade the cultural deprivation thesis proliferated until it reached into every aspect of psychological functioning, from simple perception to complex personality traits. In its broadest version, as formulated by anthropologist Oscar Lewis (1966), this thesis characterizes the whole way of life of the poor as a distinct "culture of poverty" that suffers from a marked "poverty of culture."

The deficit model has been especially influential in discussions of language development in poor black children. Often cited is the work of British sociologist Basil Bernstein (1960), who finds that class differences in modes of communication create dissimilarities in the cognitive functioning of poor and privileged children. The lower-class family uses "restricted" language codes, whereas the middle-class family uses "elaborated" structures. The "restricted" pattern is described as stereotyped and repetitive, lacking in the qualities required for exact conceptualization. In contrast, the "elaborated" language forms with which the middle-class child is familiar enable him to communicate more flexibly and precisely.

The class distinctions drawn by Bernstein and others are not limited to vocabulary, grammar, and pronunciation, but also involve processes of thought. The linguistic deficiencies of the poor are supposed to affect their power to solve problems, distinguish subtle shades of meaning, and indicate logical relationships. Thus a prominent exponent of the deficit theory, J. McVicker Hunt (1971), observes that "children in families of poverty lack many opportunities to develop cognitive skills underlying competence with language and numbers."

In support of this view, numerous studies have compared the language practices of parents in the slums and parents in the suburbs. Computers have tabulated the relative length of sentences, frequency in use of conjunctions and prepositions, and the amount of time spent in parent-child dialogue. On all such measures, it is usually found that the child of poverty is shortchanged. A number of studies by Robert Hess and his associates (1968) at the University of Chicago relate the linguistic habits and teaching styles of black mothers in different social groups to the cognitive growth of their preschool children. Middle-class black mothers rank higher than black mothers on public welfare in volume of verbal output, use of abstract words, and complexity of syntactic structures. Middle-class black children perform at higher levels on various other measures as well.* Summing up the class difference, Hunt (1971) says that "There is a world of difference between shouting simply 'shut up' and yelling 'shut up, can't you see

---

* However, Hess has elsewhere cautioned that "An unfortunate side effect of research on social class and ethnic differences is that it focuses attention upon discrepancies between groups and ignores the areas of overlap and similarity. This creates a distorted and incomplete picture . . . relatively few of the accumulated research results can be regarded as definitive" (Hess, 1970).

I am talking on the telephone.' " The child who gets the explanation along with the "shut up" presumably gets off to a better start in cognitive development.

Apart from linguistic and cognitive defects, children of the poor are said to lack the "motivational systems" needed for academic achievement and employment. Other deficiencies are found in such qualities as initiative, sense of responsibility, self-control, auditory discrimination, temporal and spatial organization, and ability to postpone gratification for longer-range rewards. Indeed, the catalogue of incapabilities attributed to the poor by author after author in the current literature is virtually limitless. The job of remedying these deficits, as now defined, would make the labors of Hercules a holiday relaxation, especially in view of the "critical periods" theory which holds that intervention may be too late to do any good after the child has reached a certain age.

The encircling gloom is deepened by Oscar Lewis' observation that "By the time slum children are six or seven they have usually absorbed the basic attitudes and values of their subculture. Thereafter they are psychologically unready to take full advantage of changing conditions or improving opportunities that may develop in their lifetime." Lewis' "culture of poverty" theory has been widely influential not only among professionals but also with the general public, thanks to such vivid books as *The Children of Sanchez* (1961) and *La Vida* (1966). While Lewis' studies dealt mainly with Puerto Ricans and Mexicans, his analysis of a self-perpetuating poverty style of life applies, he noted, to American blacks. The culture of poverty is "a subculture of Western society with its own structure and rationale," transcending national or regional differences, and exhibiting common features of family structure, interpersonal relations, and value systems. While insisting that this subculture has certain positive adaptive features, Lewis focused on such psychological characteristics as "a high incidence of weak ego structure, orality and the confusion of sexual identification, all reflecting maternal deprivation; a

strong present-time orientation with relatively little disposition to defer gratification and plan for the future, and a high
tolerance for psychological pathology of all kinds" (Lewis,
1966).

The cultural-deprivation studies, on both the psychological and sociological levels, have helped to demolish some of
the traditional myths that romanticized the lives of the poor.
These studies have forced professional workers and social scientists to look at the grim realities of slum life. But it is not
enough to look. One must also understand what one is seeing.
And genuine understanding cannot grow out of simplistic
formulas mechanically applied to complex phenomena. Unfortunately, the deficit model has encouraged such formulas.

3

As one reviews the literature on "cultural deprivation," it
becomes inescapably clear how pervasive is the premise that
the behavior, language, and thought of the poor represent deficits that are not present in the middle class. Differences are
automatically labelled deficits, particularly those of a psychological character. But differences between groups do not necessarily mean that one group has a deficit and the other an
abundance of the quality at issue. This is pointed up sharply
if one examines the differences in the language of the poor
black and the middle class. It is in the area of language that
the equation of differences and deficits has perhaps been most
prevalent.

A growing body of work (Baratz and Baratz, 1970; Stewart, 1969; Labov, 1969) is challenging the stereotype that
lower-class black children are verbally destitute and linguistically underdeveloped. The critics point out that an ethnocentric bias lies behind the assumption that linguistic competence is synonymous with the development of standard English. They cite convincing data that lower-class black children
have a fully ordered, fully structured language, differing, to
be sure, from standard English, but not by that token inferior.

"Black children are neither linguistically impoverished nor cognitively underdeveloped. Although their language system is different and, therefore, presents a handicap to any child attempting to negotiate with the standard English-speaking mainstream, it is nonetheless a fully developed, highly structured system that is more than adequate for aiding in abstract thinking" (Baratz and Baratz, 1970).

More and more language studies are coming up with findings that are contrary to conventional expectations. A Baltimore study by Doris R. Entwisle (1968), a specialist in sociolinguistics at Johns Hopkins University, found that "inner-city" black children were more advanced on certain language measures than suburban children at the time of school entrance. Similarly, children in the black ghetto of Oakland, California, "appear to acquire language at a normal rate and are clearly not 'linguistically deprived'" (Slobin, 1968). And in a Boston day-care center, lower-class black children "achieved grammatical development at a rate similar to middle-class white children" (Cazden, 1970).

Other studies have stressed the linguistic diversity among "culturally deprived" children. An investigation by Sigal and Perry (1968) of the Merrill-Palmer Institute found considerable heterogeneity among black preschool children living in a "culturally deprived area." Test results revealed a wide range of psycholinguistic competencies, and the authors rightly criticize stereotypes that blur the differences as not only derogatory but also psychologically inaccurate. Similarly, in *School Achievers from a Deprived Background,* Davidson and Greenberg (1967) point out how little publicized is the objective observation that some children from impoverished backgrounds *do* achieve satisfactorily in school. It is clearly a serious mistake to homogenize the functioning of an entire population. "Focus on the prevalence of deficiencies in the life situation of the lower class, however generously interpreted, may serve to project a fallacy as deceptive and invalid as that resulting from the earlier emphasis on the inferior intellectual potential of the lower class," observe Davidson and Greenberg. The educators conclude: "Even though we recognize that some individuals may have greater capacity than others, a dynamic view of intelligence and behavior would not consider school failure inevitable for any child. Data from experimental learning studies and the comparatively good performance of low achievers on certain tasks suggest that there is a learning potential in every child. . . . It may be that a gap will remain between the high and low achievers, but under appropriate and better controlled school experiences, no child who falls within the 'normal' range need experience failure."

The significance of such specific studies becomes clearer in the light of a recent review by Susan H. Houston (1970), a linguist at Northwestern University. Dr. Houston points out that much of the research in this field has been pursued without the requisite background of modern linguistic and psycholinguistic theory. As a result, the literature on the language of disadvantaged children is pervaded by "misconception and mythology centering around the notion of linguistic deprivation, and from this incorrect concept no useful correction programs can stem."

Citing the work of Noam Chomsky, Eric Lenneberg, and other scholars, Dr. Houston maintains that language deprivation in the traditional sense simply does not exist. There is no such thing as a "primitive" language. "All forms of all languages are systematic"; they have their own rules; and they do not differ greatly in their underlying structures. We can no longer assume that language is merely a matter of stimulus-response conditioning.

The complexity of language is not correlated with technological sophistication. Societies that function on a much simpler level of industrial development than our own have intricate linguistic structures. Certainly the inflectional features of language are not measures of cognitive processes. Modern English is less highly inflected than Anglo-Saxon, but we do not regard our speech as inferior to early English because we drop more of our noun endings to indicate case and our verb endings to indicate tense. Nor is vocabulary an infallible sign of cognitive wealth. On some vocabulary tests the slum child could easily surpass the Ph.D. candidates who now administer the exams.

The limited use of language in certain situations is not *prima facie* evidence of lack of capacity to handle language.* Children have a range of language styles, or "registers," appropriate to a given situation or environment, Dr. Houston notes. Most postulates of speech deficit in lower-class children are based on situations in which the school "register" is used, "especially when the children are black and the researcher is both white and unknown to them—and their register does give an impression of nonfluency and strange language use. But it must be borne in mind that this is neither the whole of the child's linguistic performance nor in any way representative of his linguistic competence." The fact that a child uses a different (that is, nonstandard) phonological structure doesn't necessarily mean he is "making mistakes" or is "incapable of pronouncing properly."

The contention that certain languages provide an inadequate basis for abstract thought is also highly questionable. As Dr. Houston observes, the "direction of dependence between language and cognition is still undetermined." There is no evidence that the language of the disadvantaged child does not offer as good a foundation for thinking and conceptualization as any other form of language.

This does not mean, as some have argued, that the lower-class child should not be taught standard English. On the con-

---

* The widely used Illinois Test of Psycholinguistic Abilities, designed to test language acquisition and use by children, includes the following item: "I sit on a chair; I sleep on a ——." Credit is given for responses that may include "bed, cot, couch, davenport." But some children in the rural South give such answers as "floor, rug, and chair," which correspond to the reality of their lives. Yet these children may be scored as "incorrect" (Waddell and Cahoon, 1970). Obviously the "deprivation" of the children was in not having a bed to sleep in, rather than in lacking the word "bed" or variations thereof.

trary, failure to teach it is another form of discrimination. It is a sociolinguistic fact that in our society some forms of language are an impediment to academic success and securing employment. Nonstandard language may not be "debilitating" to the child, but it can be "deleterious" (Houston, 1970).

What critics of the "deficit" theory are attacking is the failure of social scientists and educators to recognize, respect, and utilize existing cultural forms of the lower-class black community. Instead, black children are perceived as inferior and pathological. And this, as the Baratzes (1970) emphasize, represents a form of institutional racism, unwitting perhaps, but nonetheless damaging to a child who is constantly told by his teachers that everything he does, including the way he speaks, is "wrong."

Summing up "some nagging doubts" about the usefulness of "cumulative deprivation" as an explanation of educational deficiencies, two educational psychologists (Schultz and Auerbach, 1971) write: "In the face of the present, unsettled research, it is difficult to justify school programs that assume that the education deficit is intellectual, that it is caused by the lower-class environment, and that the phenomenon is permanent. These assumptions underlie characterizations such as 'deprived' and 'disadvantaged.' The logic of the self-fulfilling prophesy suggests that the use of these labels in programs designed to uplift lower-class youth ironically would have a debilitating effect. In addition, the case for permanency has been oversold in the concentration of pre-school programs. . . . Rather efforts should be devoted to the full range of elementary and secondary levels. An important component of these efforts would be a candid self-examination of teacher attitudes toward impoverished and black youth."

This caution against the educational self-fulfilling prophesy is indeed pertinent. As Rosenthal and Jacobson (1968) suggest in *Pygmalion in the Classroom,* teacher expectations of a student's intellectual development may have a significant influence on the child's school performance. Stereotypes about

the apathy and low mental ability of the black student help
to determine their behavior. Discrimination contributes to
the "inferiority," which is then used to rationalize the
discrimination.

4

If the deficit model holds up so poorly with regard to language, which can be studied with some precision, it becomes
an especially frail foundation for theories about broader behavioral characteristics. Behavior must always be viewed in
terms of its adaptive function in a given life setting. Since the
conditions of life among the poor are drastically different from
those among the middle class, their behavior has to be significantly different. Otherwise, an individual would find it difficult
or impossible to function effectively within his own socio-
economic group. When Hunt (1971) and others talk about
the poor lacking initiative, motivation, self-control, etc., they
are clearly evaluating such attributes according to the way
they manifest themselves in middle-class adaptations. But the
same characteristics appear very differently in youngsters
growing up in the slums. Unless one asks oneself, "Motivation
for what purpose, initiative for what goal, self-control in what
circumstances?" the categories themselves become abstract
and inapplicable in the evaluation of different social groups.

In *Children of Crisis*, Coles (1967) effectively refutes the
deeply rooted notion—or prejudice, to call it by its right name
—that children who come from a background of poverty are
likely to be emotionally blighted. He describes the resilience
and toughness and ingenuity displayed by many such children
in the South. And in the ghettos of the North as well he finds
exuberance and vitality in young children. "Such children
come to school prepared to be active, vigorous, perhaps much
more outgoing on the average than middle-class children. But
they are quick to lose patience, sulk, feel wrong or wronged
and cheated by a world they have learned to be impossible,
uncertain, and contradictory."

The deficit concept has also been too mechanically applied
to perception. Thus some authors maintain that black children
in the ghetto have low auditory discrimination. Because of the
excessive noise in their environment they learn to be inatten-
tive, and this "defect" has been implicated in their poor reading ability. But another interpretation is possible. As one
psychologist (Gordon, 1968) has suggested, "Such auditory
functioning may also serve as part of what Hemingway praised
as a 'built-in shockproof crap detector,' that from a positive
point of view it might function to enable disadvantaged kids
to concentrate and perform well in noisy environments by
screening out interfering sounds, and that such a skill might
therefore be made to function as an asset were the classroom
to reward it and see it as a skill required in an increasingly
noise-polluted urban environment."

Above and beyond such issues, one must also question the
presumption and arrogance of the premise that the white
middle-class way is a desirable one. At this point in history, it
hardly needs belaboring that the established middle-class mores
are not providing a healthy basis for the flourishing of humanistic values. One can hardly pick up a book or article by a
thoughtful observer of American life without an anguished
reminder of this truth.

Moreover, the preoccupation with psychological "deprivation" has dulled a concern for those deficits that do plague the
life of the poor and urgently require correction—health and
nutrition, housing, schools, and job opportunity. We would
especially emphasize the issue of health and nutrition because
so much that has been attributed to psychological deprivation
has really been due to physiological factors. There has been a
serious underestimation of the impact of poor health and nutrition on school failure, as Birch and Gussow (1970) point
out in their assessment of the effect of poverty on the intellectual potential of children. "The same homes which lack toys
and games are the homes in which hunger and disease abound,"
they observe. The focus on "cognitive understimulation" in

such homes all too often beclouds their central and urgent
need for adequate food and medical care.

5

One psychological premise of the cultural deprivation theory is that there are "critical periods" of mental growth. At
certain stages of a child's development, it is argued, he must
be exposed to specific learning experiences. If these experiences
are absent, the child is presumed to suffer a permanent intellectual deficit. Once the learning opportunity is missed, the
child will never reach his full cognitive potential. By the time
he is of school age, it is "already too late."

This hypothesis is "sometimes presented as a proved fact,
though there is no persuasive evidence at present to support
it," notes Dr. Peter H. Wolff (1970), a Harvard psychiatrist
and leading investigator in child development. "Its acceptance
by educators, psychologists, and some physicians has filtered
down to parents, some of whom, when they see their children
lagging behind others in academic achievement, may blame
themselves for not doing enough to enrich their children during
critical periods." By blaming the home and preschool environment for a child's learning difficulties it becomes easier to
bypass the need for reconstruction of the schools.

To a large extent, the "critical periods" theorists base
themselves on an analogy with early "imprinting" in various
animal species. But as Dr. Wolff points out, the tranposition
of behavioral mechanisms from selected species of lower animals to human behavior has been all too facile and mechanical.
In children "we may state with some assurance that there is
no evidence for biologically fixed critical periods of cognitive
development."

Supporters of the critical periods hypothesis sometimes
cite Benjamin Bloom's finding in *Stability and Change in
Human Characteristics* (1964) that intelligence loses its plas-
ticity after about four years of age. Bloom suggests that the
environment has more impact on a psychological characteristic

at a time when the characteristic is undergoing rapid change—
that is, in infancy and early childhood. Often overlooked, however, is the fact that a child's environment is likely to continue
essentially unchanged as he grows older. The psychological
consequences of his earliest conditions are perpetuated and
reinforced. Thus the apparent stability of a child's traits may
be due to constancy of environment at least as much as to intrapsychic stability. As Bloom himself points out, "Our research suggests that although the environment may have its
greatest effect on individuals in the first year or so that they
are within it, its effect is stabilized and reinforced only when
the environment is relatively constant over a period of time."
Continuing poverty and discrimination will have self-duplicat-
ing effects. But this is a far cry from the theory that it is no
use to offer expanded opportunities after the preschool age.

To question the critical period concept is not to deny the
possibility of differences in learning ease at various age periods.
But at what specific stages do different learning rates occur?
Is the optimum learning period the same for all children? And
is the optimum period the same for all kinds of learning? These
are important issues for educational psychology to explore.
Existing data are quite inadequate, though a number of studies
provide "evidence for multiple mental abilities, which develop
in different ways. Some show more continuous growth than
others. Some are more consistent over time than others . . ."
(Bayley, 1970). The hypothesis of critical periods, with its
absolutistic rejection of such differences, actually serves to
inhibit rather than to stimulate the kind of study needed in
this field.

6

On the sociological level, many serious questions have been
raised about the "culture of poverty" hypothesis (H. Lewis,
1967; Rodman, 1968; Valentine, 1968; Ryan, 1971). Authoritative studies of poverty areas in Washington, D. C., conducted
by black sociologist Hylan Lewis reveal a "wide variety in

the styles of individuals and families." After a detailed investigation of child-rearing practices, Hylan Lewis emphasizes that "the amount and the implications of the diversity among Negroes in low-income urban families are too frequently overlooked and underrated in popular and scientific thinking." One effect of linking "culture" and "class," he observes, is the tendency "to impute to a total category, such as the lower class, the depreciated, and probably the more dramatic and threatening, characteristics of a segment of that category" (Lewis, 1967).

In a comprehensive critique of the "culture of poverty" literature, Charles A. Valentine, a University of Chicago anthropologist, notes that ill-founded conclusions about the poor, based on inadequate research, are influencing public policy in a pernicious way. Valentine does not contend that cultural distinctions confined to the poor are either theoretically impossible or factually nonexistent. But he does believe that social scientists like Nathan Glazer and Daniel Patrick Moynihan view the poor with a built-in bias. As a result of this bias, "the principal causes of the plight of the poor are found in the internal deficiencies of their own way of life, and their total condition is seen as not only self-perpetuating, but essentially hopeless" (Valentine, 1968).

Valentine stresses the need to distinguish between cultural values and situational or circumstantial adaptations. It is a misconception "that people live as they do because they prefer their actual mode of existence and its consequences." In a highly stratified social system like that of the United States, poor people have a narrow margin of choice as to how they will live. It is risky indeed to infer a group's preferences and potentialities from the adaptations forced upon them by their conditions of existence. Such inferences inevitably result in what William Ryan, Professor of Psychology at Boston College, so aptly terms "Blaming the Victim." He writes: "Briefly, 'Blaming the Victim' is an intellectual process whereby a social problem is analyzed in such a way that the causation is found

to be in the qualities and characteristics of the victim rather
than in any deficiencies or structural defects in the environment" (Ryan, 1971).

In raising questions about the "deficit" approach, we do
not wish to be misunderstood. We are not suggesting that it
is great to be poor. But we are saying that it is bad enough
to be poor and to suffer the real deprivations of poverty without being saddled with imaginary and irremediable psychological defects.

6
Family and Fantasy

THE STRONG INFLUENCE of the family on personality development has properly received increasing attention in recent years. But this influence is often viewed in a simplistic way and crudely overstated. Family "permissiveness" is cited as the cause of the youth rebellion against the war in Vietnam and social hypocrisy. The "schizophrenogenic" mother is blamed for a child's psychotic behavior. Family psychotherapy, useful in certain instances, is proclaimed by enthusiasts as a universally essential procedure.

This intense focus on the family as the determinant of pathology or health may encourage serious misconceptions— the assumption, for example, that a certain type of family pattern always has the same consequences. Actually, of course, there is no one-to-one relation between family structure and personality development. A family may have a weak father and a dominant mother, or an authoritarian father and submissive mother; yet in each situation the impact on children of different temperament may be quite diverse. The broken home does not necessarily breed delinquency; nor does the intact home assure socially approved behavior. Loving mothers may have emotionally disturbed children, and disturbed mothers may have well-adapted children who are apparently immune to the mother's pathology and erratic patterns of care.

To be sure, it is more usual for emotionally healthy parents to have healthy children, and for the emotionally ill to have children with problems. But this is by no means inevitable. "There is not a direct quantitative relationship between pathology in a parent and pathology in a child," observes Dr. Helen Beiser (1964) of the Institute for Juvenile Research in Chicago. It is therefore hazardous to generalize about the influence of the family on children.

This truth is especially pertinent to black families. These families have been given far less systematic study than have white middle-class families, but they are the subject of even more sweeping generalizations.

The most glaring example is the widely publicized Moynihan Report, *The Negro Family: The Case for National Action,* issued by the U.S. Department of Labor in 1965.* The report describes the black family as a "tangle of pathology." It contrasts the "approaching complete breakdown" of Negro families with the enduring solidity of their white counterparts. "The white family," says the Moynihan Report, "has achieved a high degree of stability and is maintaining that stability."

Implicit in this assertion are several false premises. To begin with, the conception of a homogeneous and perdurable "white family" is manifestly groundless. This hypothetical entity cannot be abstracted from a specific setting of class, religion, cultural background, time, and interpersonal variations. Many volumes have been written on the differences in the living patterns and values of rural and urban families, 19th-century and 20th-century families, immigrant and second-generation families, lower-class and upper-class families. What do the migratory workers of Steinbeck's *The Grapes of Wrath* have in common with the urban aristocrats of Edith Wharton's novels, apart from the color of their skin? The authoritarian patriarchy of the Victorian era has yielded to less rigid relationships. And every unhappy family is unhappy in its own way, as Tolstoy reminds us in *Anna Karenina.*

---

* For the text of this report and comment by various authors, see Rainwater and Yancey (1967).

A second assumption of the Moynihan Report is that the hypothetical "white family" may appropriately serve as a model against which all other families may be measured. Even if it were possible to encompass the white family in Moynihan's confident generalizations, why should it serve as a paradigm of satisfactory functioning? There are many other living styles. Only an embattled parochialism will ignore the diverse cultural patterns in the world and the viability of families that differ in fundamental respects from the American white middle-class model. They may be more closely or more loosely knit, more repressive or more permissive, more child-centered or more respectful of elders. It is arrogantly ethnocentric to judge other cultures according to the degree to which they deviate from one's own.

Moreover, it is erroneous to assume that the "white family" model actually possesses the virtues attributed to it in the Moynihan Report. How valid, for example, is the assertion that this family is maintaining "a high degree of stability?" The main indices of stability used by the Report are divorce and illegitimacy. But judged by these indices, American families in general are not flourishing. "White divorce rates have zoomed almost 800 per cent in less than 100 years, and white illegitimacy has increased more than 50 per cent in the last twenty-five years—a rate of increase greater than that of Negroes," observed psychologist William Ryan (1965) in a trenchant analysis of the Moynihan Report. The current psychiatric literature is replete with studies of malfunctioning white families.* The "generation gap" is often a euphemism for sharp family dislocation. And the rapidly rising rate of

* A leading authority on the family, psychiatrist Nathan W. Ackerman (1970), catalogued the maladies afflicting the family in modern Western society: "1. A form of family anomie, reflected in a lack of consensus on values, a disturbance in identity-relations and a pervasive sense of powerlessness; 2. Chronic immaturity, the inability to assume effective responsibility and an impaired potential for viable family growth; 3. Discontinuity and incongruity in the relations between family and society." In light of this, why the focus on *black* family pathology?

drug addiction and alcoholism in white suburbia hardly testifies to the stability which black families should seek to emu-
late. The model itself is an illusion.

The lopsided emphasis on the black family as characteris-
tically a broken family or "approaching complete breakdown"
nourishes the stereotype of ethnic blight. The reality is different: the "typical" black family, in the sense of the commonest,
is the one in which both husband and wife are living together
in their first marriage (Bernard, 1966; Farley and Hermalin,
1971). The selective focus on "disorganization" helps perpetuate the myth that black people feel less close to members of
their family than do white persons. And whether the pathology
of family life is attributed to the background of slavery and
oppression or to some inherent instability in the black psyche,
the end result is the same. It is to make "family breakdown"
a peculiarly racial phenomenon. The onus is placed on the
black family as a self-perpetuating source of pathology, rather
than on the racist society which condemns most blacks to poverty, slum housing, and inferior schools.

An authoritative report by the Joint Commission on Mental Health of Children (1970) noted that "The most important
single factor associated with family breakdown is poverty
itself." Among both white and black families there is a definite
relationship between being poor and living in a family from
which the father is absent. In 1964, three times as many
white families with a female head had incomes below the
poverty line than did white families with a male head. Among
black families more than twice as many families with absent
fathers lived below the poverty line than did those where the
father was present. In both white and black families the rates
of illegitimacy, divorce, and separation increase as one goes
down the socioeconomic scale. Strongly associated with family
breakdowns are such factors as high unemployment rate of
low-income men, poor health, inadequate housing, low-grade
education, large families. All these factors are aggravated in
poor black families.

However, the fact that proportionally more blacks than whites are poor has often led to the judgment that blacks themselves are responsible for their poverty. As Billingsley (1968) notes in a review of American scholarship on black families, "Seeking to explain only *Negro* poverty, one could conveniently ignore the mass of causal factors and focus on the Negro people themselves, their leadership, their psychological motivation and aspirations, their family structure, and, in a flash of superficial enlightenment, their history of slavery." As a result, most studies focusing on the problem-ridden sectors of black family life are really not concerned with black family life at all. "They are concerned, instead, with poverty, family breakdown, and illegitimacy, and somehow tie these phenomena to the Negro experience. This seems to obviate, for a time at least, the urgent need to explain these phenomena in the larger white society. . . . This can postpone for a time the possible revelation that these pathologies may be endemic to our society, and are therefore normative and structural— not merely functions of individual, psychological and subcultural hangups."

2

Basic to the "tangle of pathology" thesis is the description of the black family as "matriarchal." This tag has by force of repetition acquired the authority of unassailable truth. "In essence," says the Moynihan Report, "the Negro community has been forced into a matriarchal structure which, because it is so out of line with the rest of American society, seriously retards the progress of the group as a whole, and imposes a crushing burden on the Negro male and, in consequence, on a great many women as well." Maternal domination is the "fearful price" that black Americans have paid for their mistreatment by whites over the centuries. This view, in general,

is the one propounded in such influential psychiatric books as
Theodore Lidz' *The Person* (1968).*

The thesis has a certain plausibility since it appears to be
rooted in history. Under slavery, the black family did indeed
sustain heavy blows. "In Africa," Stampp (1956) notes, "the
Negroes had been accustomed to a strictly regulated family
life and a rigidly enforced moral code. But in America the
disintegration of their social organization removed the traditional sanctions which had encouraged them to respect their
old customs." The white masters, though reared in proper
patriarchal settings, did not recognize the legality of marriage
between blacks. Chattels could not make contracts—even, the
churches added, to satisfy the ordinances of divinity. The
Supreme Court of North Carolina ruled that "The relation
between slaves is entirely different from that of man and wife
joined in lawful wedlock," since "with slaves it may be dis-
solved at the pleasure of either party, or by the sale of one
or both, depending on the caprice or necessity of the owners."
So families were broken up at the convenience and profit of
the defenders of white civilization—to raise money for paying
a gambling debt or to buy a new horse. Under such circumstances, said one owner of human property, it was "far more
humane not to cherish ties among slaves."

But the humane efforts of the slaveholders to erase feelings
of kinship and affection did not succeed. The heartbreak of
forced separation from loved ones was not a fiction concocted
by sentimental Abolitionists. Family feeling is movingly documented in innumerable narratives by ex-slaves, written and
oral. The agony of the auction block was described by Josiah
Henson, whose account of his life was a sourcebook for Harriet
Beecher Stowe: "The first sad announcement that the sale is
to be; the knowledge that all ties of the past are to be sun-
dered; the frantic terror at the idea of being sent 'down

---

* Lidz observes that "Matriarchy, or at least the mother-centered
family, became a pattern that tends to persist, affording the boy an
inadequate role pattern to follow into manhood."

south'; the almost certainty that one member of a family will be torn from another; the anxious scanning of purchasers' faces; the agony at parting, often forever, with husband, wife, child—these must be seen and felt to be fully understood. Young as I was then, the iron entered into my soul."

Whatever "stability" a family could achieve in these conditions depended largely on the mother. The man's role as husband and father was systematically denied. But to speak of this form of family life as "matriarchal" is surely to invite confusion. Matriarchy implies power, and it is a mockery to think in such terms when considering the black family under slavery. Power was vested in the slaveholder, not in the mother. She could make no independent decision about her child's existence or her relation to a husband. Indeed she had little power even to determine the use of her body when it served the pleasure of its legal owner.

"That the Negro American has survived at all is extraordinary—a lesser people might simply have died out, as others have," as the Moynihan Report correctly notes. But instead of seeking to understand the sources of black strength, Moynihan exaggerates black vulnerability. Instead of viewing the black family in terms of the adaptive strategies that enabled it to survive, the Report characterizes this family's departures from "the rest of American society" as evidence of pathology. The conventional judgment of the black family locks it into a hopeless contradiction: without "matriarchy," no survival; with "matriarchy," no health.

This concept, long dominant in the social science literature, has come under sharp scrutiny by a number of investigators (Valentine, 1968; Billingsley, 1968; Staples, 1970; Herzog and Lewis, 1970; TenHouten, 1970; Ladner, 1971). They have taken a fresh look at the "matriarchy" assumption, re-examined the presumed evidence, and come up with new conclusions. Many long-accepted generalizations about the black family have turned out to be myths, or at least gross over-simplifications. And this implies, as we shall see, the need to reconsider certain ideas about black personality and psychopathology that were predicated on the "matriarchy" thesis.

This thesis has been challenged on two basic counts. First, the validity of the description: Is the so-called role reversal of husband and wife the characteristic pattern of the black family? Second, the interpretation of such evidence as we have: Does a "mother-dominated" home necessarily breed pathology?

The matriarchy theorists usually specify that they are referring only to the low-income family (that is, the vast majority of black families). The Moynihan Report, for example, cites the observation of Franklin Frazier's *Black Bourgeoisie* that "the middle-class Negro American family is, if anything, more patriarchal and protective of its children than the general run of such families."

But recent studies of lower-class black families emphasize that these cannot be categorized in terms of a single structure. Three types of patterning associated with authority and decision-making are described by Billingsley (1968): "There are the vanishing *patriarchies,* where men make most of the decisions in crucial areas of family life. They form a minority among low-income Negro families, but they still exist to some extent. Then there are the resilient *matriarchies* in which the wife and mother exerts an inordinate amount of authority at the expense of or in the absence of the husband and father. This is the second most common authority pattern among low-income Negro families, and not the most common as is often assumed. Then, finally, there are the expanding *equalitarians.* These are the families in which both husband and wife participate actively and jointly in decision making in the major areas of family life. Their tribes are increasing at the expense of both the patriarchy and the matriarchy. This is the most common pattern of authority among lower class Negro families today."*

---

* These findings were re-affirmed in a report on *The Strengths of Black Families* issued by the National Urban League at its annual

Low-income black families do not regard as either desirable or inevitable a family pattern in which the woman is dominant. "On the contrary," Elizabeth Herzog and Hylan Lewis (1970) observe in a perceptive review, "the accepted ideal norm, in ghetto as in Gold Coast, is a stable marriage in which the man is the chief breadwinner, and the so-called Negro matriarchs are the first to decry the perfidy of the male who does not fulfill this role." The black mother does not seek or welcome dominance. It merely adds to her burdens and responsibilities. As Grier and Cobbs (1968) note, "The simplistic view of the black family as a matriarchy is an unfortunate theme repeated too often by scholars who should know better. If a man is stripped of his authority in the home by forces outside that home, the woman naturally must assume the status of head of household. This is the safety factor inherent in a household which includes two adults and it by no means suggests that the woman prefers it that way. If a woman is widowed she may assume many masculine functions, but the household may be a patriarchy without a patriarch."

The fact that black women have the main responsibility for child-rearing does not distinguish them from American mothers in general. "In fact," say Herzog and Lewis (1970), "a good deal of hand-wringing is devoted to the pervasiveness of women in the lives of middle-income and upper-income white children, and the ascribed effects of this pervasiveness. On the split level, it is called momism. We seem to reserve the matriarchal label for ethnic minorities viewed across a social distance." And in working-class families, whether black or white, it is even more true that mothers have the main child-rearing responsibility.

---

convention in July, 1971. The report was prepared by sociologist Robert B. Hill, the organization's associate director of research, who told newsmen that "Our own lives taught us that these things social scientists were telling us were not true. If, as most scholars agree, there is a need to strengthen black families, then a first order of priority should be the identification of presently existing strengths" (*N. Y. Times*, July 27, 1971).

It is often assumed that black husbands leave their wives in order to avoid their subordinate role in the family. The father's absence is attributed to his recoil against emasculation. But there is no evidence to support such an assumption. An extensive review of the literature by TenHouten (1970), a UCLA sociologist, concludes: "The methodologies used in studies of family power structure vary considerably, which hampers comparison of existing research. Further, there exists no single measure of female dominance that is known to be reliable and valid, and is widely used. The weight of existing evidence, however, suggests that the stereotype of lower-class black families as matriarchal, pathological, and 'approaching a state of complete breakdown,' may in reality constitute social mythology. The reality is that such a view is not supported by a convincing body of social research."

3

But even if there were more evidence to support the matriarchal stereotype, would this prove that "mother domination" is the major source of personality disorder? There is a persistent tendency to trace the emotional problems of children to harmful maternal attitudes. This tendency, aptly called the *mal de mère* syndrome (Chess, 1964), is exemplified in child-guidance clinics that habitually consider a child's behavior problem as directly reactive to maternal handling. In a "mother-dominated" family the maternal influence is presumably all the more noxious since it is unchecked by a strong male figure.

Thus, in a study of 19 neurotic black children in Baltimore, psychiatrist Eugene B. Brody (1963) asserts: "It seems unlikely that a relationship with a mother as the most important power, however secure, can be an adequate basis for the development of a stable social identity in a boy, whether in terms of sex, color, or other significant element." Such conjectures have not been validated. They are based on small clinical samples. And because they are clinical samples, they involve

children who already have a disturbance sufficiently serious
to bring them to psychiatric attention. Left out of the reckon-
ing are all those children reared in mother-dominated families
who have not developed any disorder. The fact is that there
are no detailed longitudinal studies of large random samples
drawn from presumably pathogenic black families. There are
no full-scale studies that take into account the many variations in the patterns of relationships with mothers, the individual personalities of both the mothers and the children, and
the specific circumstances that have produced the matrifocal
family.

Another problem is the unexamined assumption about the
mother's "power." It may be questioned whether any child
growing up in a ghetto comes to view his mother as an all-
powerful figure, or even as the "most important" power. Quite
early the child learns that in specific and basic areas of functioning his mother is less powerful than the welfare social
worker, the policeman, the landlord, or the teacher. The issue
of power is too often posed by social scientists in strictly
intrafamilial terms. The family appears to exist in a social
vacuum. But family structure is not an absolute; it can be
understood only in its interaction with the larger society.

Brody is aware of this. He cites *The Mark of Oppression*
as providing evidence that the black man has had a problem
maintaining his masculine status not only because of the family structure but also because of the "emasculating pressure"
of the white society. He writes: "The hypothetical emasculation may begin with the little boy's awareness that his father
and father-surrogates are vulnerable in relation to white
males" (Brody, 1961). But what about the vulnerability of the
black mother? Somehow she generally finds herself linked with
her oppressors as an "emasculating" force.

Black mothers are also blamed for confusing their children
with contradictory messages about the world outside the family. Brody asserts that black youngsters receive conflicting
cues: On the verbal level, "Your opportunities are good"; on

the non-verbal: "You really don't have a chance." There is also said to be a gulf between the conscious and unconscious message. The conscious message is to the effect that "People are all the same inside," while simultaneously the unconscious message, transmitted through affective and behavior cues, is essentially: "While I tell you that people are the same inside, I expect you to behave as though this is not true, and, in fact, I don't believe it myself."

This concept is reminiscent of the "double-bind" theory advanced by Gregory Bateson as a cause of schizophrenia. According to this theory, the patient is caught in an "unescapable double bind" of conflicting messages from important members of his family. A parent may verbally assert his love for the patient, but at the same time manifest tension that conveys an unspoken hatred. Such distorted intrafamilial communication presumably fosters a schizophrenic breakdown.

Whatever the merit of the theory in general, its application to black children needs to be most carefully evaluated. In Brody's study, for example, the interviewers were white, which he concedes "poses an obvious methodological problem." It does indeed. Is it not possible that the black mother's "message" has been misread by the white researcher rather than by the children themselves? Moreover, the mother's apparently contradictory message may be an accurate transmission of the ambiguities of social reality. The black mother's danger signals may not be "unconscious" at all, but quite deliberate. She could hardly help her child cope with reality if she failed to communicate the hazards, often mortal, of his environment. At the same time, simply to issue warnings without some dimension of hope and encouragement might well make the message less conflictual but actually more damaging. The mother, as we see in the stories of Langston Hughes or in Lorraine Hansberry's *A Raisin in the Sun,* may be a much more complex and subtle conveyor of reality than she is usually given credit for.

The "baneful influence" of black mothers is especially

visible in psychoanalytic discussions. Typical is an oft-cited
article by Sclare (1953) on "Cultural Determinants in the
Neurotic Negro." It offers three case studies considered "representative of a large class of problems" in black American
men. In all three patients "unconscious feminine trends were
pronounced, and the patients tended to utilize pseudo-masculine defenses, such as alcoholism, reckless behavior, etc." And
the source of the difficulty is not far to seek: it is the "regres-
sive" family structure that persists among working-class
Negroes. The mother "tends to be infantilizing and over-pro-
tective towards her children who, while receiving maximal
gratification at the oral phase of development, are usually subjected to prohibitive, demanding or threatening attitudes at
the anal and phallic levels. They are thus obstructed on the
road to maturity."

Thus the so-called immaturity or infantilism of the black
is not ascribed, as in the past, to the Biblical "Curse of Ham"
or to lower evolutionary development, but to the mother.

A different psychiatric perspective is offered by Grier and
Cobbs (1968). They observe that black men often link their
own repressed feelings with both the restrictive mother and
the inhibiting society. Their anger may at first be directed at
both. Later, however, there comes "a deeper understanding of
the mother as a concerned mediator between society and the
child. The patient comes to recognize that, while the larger
society imposes a harsh inhibition on his development and a
threat to any aggressivity, the hostility of society is communicated to him by his mother, whose primary concern is that he
survive. For if he does not realize that his aggressiveness puts
him in grave danger from society generally, he may *not* survive. With this recognition his hostility toward his mother
lessens and is directed toward white society."

To view the black mother only as a repressor of rebellion
and aggressivity is therefore to adopt a stereotype. Actually she
has played and continues to play a leading part in the liberation movement. As Jeanne L. Noble (1966), a black woman

leader, writes: "One can walk into any church on 'Movement Night' in the South and see hundreds of Negro women singing, exulting and putting hard-earned coins into the collection plates. They march, kneel-in, go to jail and do many of the chores necessary to keep a protest movement going." In a study of life styles in the black ghetto, McCord and Howard (1969) found that a large proportion of the women in Houston and Watts shared the views of men on the major issues facing them and the means to fight the white establishment. It appears that "women in Negro society are not exerting the 'pacifying' influence that one might expect"—or be led to expect by much of the social science literature.

Stereotypes about black women have also been powerfully refuted by Joyce A. Ladner, a sociologist at the Institute of the Black World in Atlanta. In her book *Tomorrow's Tomorrow: The Black Woman,* based on extensive research in an all-black, low-income housing project in St. Louis, Dr. Ladner (1971) presents evidence of healthy coping with unhealthy conditions. The book is eloquent testimony to the courage and strength of black women, and it persuasively demonstrates that "studies which have as their focal point the alleged deviant *attitudes* and *behavior* of Blacks are grounded within the racist assumptions and principles that only render Blacks open to further exploitation."

Another black sociologist, Dr. Robert Staples of the University of California, Irvine, suggests that the stereotype of the domineering black woman, hated by her sons, is "a cruel hoax" propagated as part of a divide-and-conquer strategy. In his trenchant essay on "The Myth of the Black Matriarchy," Dr. Staples (1970) says that "It has been functional for the white ruling class, through its ideological apparatus, to create internal antagonisms between black men and women to divide them and to ward off effective attacks on the external system of white racism." This author notes that if black women possess any "inordinate power" it is due to the barriers set up to the employment of black males, often making it necessary for the woman to be the main breadwinner. The black woman's self-reliance "has been a necessary trait in order for her and her children to survive in a racist and hostile society."

4

As a corollary of the "matriarchy" thesis, many authors maintain that the absence of a male authority figure in the family makes it hard for children to distinguish between male and female roles. Boys identify with their mothers and adopt feminine characteristics, while girls take on attitudes associated with the male responsibilities assumed by the mother. The presumed confusion of sex identity is supposed to have harmful effects on psychological development, particularly of boys. Several studies have emphasized that "father-deprived boys are markedly more immature, submissive, dependent and effeminate than other boys both in their overt behavior and fantasies" (Pettigrew, 1964). As they grow up, the boys with cross-sex identity may compensate by taking on an exaggerated masculinity and adopting a facade of toughness.

This theory has been repeatedly applied to black families. Some investigators have reported that lower-class black males register higher than their white counterparts on personality measures of femininity. In a comparison of two groups of adult working-class blacks in Boston, Pettigrew (1964) noted that manifestations of disturbed sexual identification were more frequent among those whose father had been absent during their childhood. Psychiatric reports, such as the one by Sclare already cited, have reported that behaviorally disturbed black men exhibit a relatively high prevalence of "pseudo-masculine defenses."

But studies dealing with masculinity and femininity tend to employ criteria that are subjective and vague. Whether based on a questionnaire or a tiny clinical sample, the findings often reflect the preconceptions of the observer. One of the most widely used personality tests, the Minnesota Multiphasic

Inventory (MMPI), asks a respondent to indicate whether statements apply to him. Rated as a "feminine" sign is the choice of such statements as "I would like to be a singer" and "I think I feel more intensely than most people do." Another test, the California Personality Inventory, gives a low-femininity rating to girls who do not fear thunderstorms or do not wish to be librarians, while a low-masculinity rating is reserved for boys who express no desire to drive a racing car or to read *Popular Mechanics* (Vincent, 1966).

Both the content and interpretation of such tests have been sharply challenged. In a careful review, Herzog and Sudia (1968) report that while a preponderance of relevant research suggests lower masculinity scores on the part of "fatherless" boys, the verdict is less decisive if one considers only studies rated reasonably sound in method. In any event, there is much overlap between the children of one-parent and two-parent homes, and the mean scores of the groups compared show only a moderate difference.

Studies of sex-role confusion have rightly been criticized for being class-bound, culture-bound, and time-bound. Often cited in the literature on this subject is a study of Norwegian boys whose sailor-fathers shipped out for long periods of time. This study, as Herzog and Lewis (1970) point out, "has been held up as demonstrating what can be expected for fatherless boys in Harlem. . . . This kind of generalization is dubious in itself. It appears the more questionable in light of a careful replication in Italy that produced findings in flat contradiction to those obtained in Norway."

The investigator who has an *a priori* theory about the effect of the "fatherless" family on a black man can easily accommodate contradictory data. A low masculinity score may be taken as a sign of feminization, a high score as a sign of overcompensation. Clinical judgment too can easily be distorted by a schematic approach to sex-identity confusion presumably arising from the mother-dominated home.

It is a mistake to assume that children, especially boys,

must have a specific father figure to serve as a role model for ✓
sex identification. Actually, as Herzog and Sudia note, "children learn about maleness and femaleness from many sources, including adults in their homes, their peer group, TV, movies, and other mass media, and especially the persons—children or adults—who influence them particularly." While there may not be a male figure in the nuclear family, there may be several in the extended family. But even without male figures close to the family, it is possible for many mothers, depending on their own understanding and emotional maturity, to help their children develop an appropriate sex identity.

Significantly, there is a growing awareness on the part of adoption agencies that placement of a child in a one-parent family is not necessarily a bad idea. This would once have been considered unthinkable because psychological harm to the child would be inevitable. But the rising number of "hard-to-place" children has spurred some agencies to reevaluate the traditional taboo against adoption by a single parent (Branham, 1970). In 1965 the Los Angeles County Department of Adoptions began to place children—predominantly black, Mexican-American, and mixed-parentage babies for whom no other homes could be found—with persons having no marital partner in their home.

One may agree that, all other things being equal, the two-parent family is more desirable. But other things are not always equal. There are two-parent families that in theory are "intact" but are in reality torn apart by unhealthy incompatibilities. There are one-parent families that in theory are "broken" but actually function in a normal and productive way. The two-parent family is not a guarantee against confusion of sex roles, and the one-parent family does not inevitably generate such confusion.

That black families in America face special problems goes without saying, but it is a mistake to assume that these problems have been met in the same way by all black families and all black mothers. The dilemmas of socialization in a racist society can indeed be cruel. "How Negro parents have resolved these dilemmas is a virtually untouched field of study," as Billingsley (1968) points out. "While Negro families have informally shared their experiences with one another, the startling neglect of such important areas of expressive functioning in Negro family life finds us without information which is vital to understanding not only the Negro family, but also a very rich part of the human experience."

In the absence of detailed, scientifically controlled studies, it is nothing less than racist to generalize about the "pathologic" black family and the "castrating" black mother. The tendency to parrot such stereotypes can only encourage the superstition of white superiority.

7

The Sexual Mystique

<hr>

I

A PREOCCUPATION with the sexual theme haunts both the popular and professional literature on black-white relationships. The hangup is unmistakable. And it is scarcely surprising in view of our national history. From the earliest days of slavery, whites have exploited black men and women as objects of sexual interest. It is in the tumultuous realm of sexuality that racist thinking achieves its most spectacular topsy-turviness. White men forced black women into their beds—and cried "Rape" when a black man so much as glanced at White Womanhood on her pedestal of chastity. White men fathered black children—and asserted that there was a "natural repugnance" between the races. Whites castrated black men— and proclaimed that they were thus defending the values of Western civilization.

In no other area of human experience have the distortions of racism been more bizarre. The fantasies of white people endowed blacks with extraordinary genitalia and sexual prowess. As far back as the 16th century, Englishmen were ascribing to Africans, known to them only by hearsay, an unrestrained lustfulness to which Othello's enemies referred ("the gross clasps of the lascivious Moor"). A 17th-century traveler described to a popeyed audience the "large Propagators" of African men, and an early slaver advertised the "hot constitution'd Ladies" in his cargo. Even so relatively enlightened

101

a slaveowner as Thomas Jefferson echoed the concept of blacks
as primitively sensual beings, observing in *Notes on Virginia*
that "They are more ardent after their female; but love seems
with them to be more an eager desire than a tender delicate
mixture of sentiment and sensation." An essential part of the
myth is that black women are promiscuously yielding to white
men, and that black men uniformly hunger for white women.
This myth is even employed retroactively, as in William
Styron's treatment of a black hero in his novel *The Confessions of Nat Turner*. As psychiatrist Alvin F. Poussaint (1968)
has pointed out, "Styron presents a Caucasian stereotype of
the black man's innermost desires, which is to sexually possess
a white woman."

The sexual potency and abandon attributed to blacks was
not considered admirable (even if some might argue that this
was the "unconscious" meaning) but rather as still another
mark of their inferiority in the human family. The stereotype
was associated with "the sexuality of beasts and the bestiality
of sex," notes a leading historian of white attitudes (Jordan,
1968). The presumed hypersexuality of blacks was "merely
another attribute that one would expect to find among heathen,
savage, beast-like men." In this country during the last century, physicians were a major source of the "scientific" argument that the Negro's "sexual extremes belong to the age of
awakening consciousness or nascent intelligence, a stage of
incipience to moral and intellectual development," as Dr. W.
T. English of Pittsburgh wrote in 1903 (Haller, 1970a). The
specter of black rape inhabited the pages of major medical
journals. One professor at the Chicago College of Physicians
warned that "the *furor sexualis* in the Negro resembles similar
sexual attacks in the bull and elephant, and the running amuck
of the Malay race." Physicians feared attacks on the white
woman's body, "a holy temple dedicated by God, in which
alone may continue the ever complicating warp and woof of
evolution."

There was only one way to protect that holy temple. "To

deal with the animal passions of the Negro, doctors prescribed castration," reports historian John Haller (1970a) in his study of medical sources, "The Physician Versus the Negro." As Dr. G. Frank Lydston of Chicago argued in 1893, "A few emasculated Negroes scattered around through the thickly-settled Negro communities would really prove the conservation of energy, as far as the repression of sexual crimes is concerned."

What is the essential meaning of all these fantasies of hypersexuality and prescriptions of castration? The answer has been suggested by a black sociologist, Calvin C. Hernton (1965, 1971). "Whether intentional or not" he observes, "the white world's definition of Negro sexuality has served to frustrate and arrest the political struggle of black people throughout the years, especially in the South where oppression and racism have been most brutal. The sexualization of racism (or the racism of sex) as a *political* instrument to be used against the liberation of black people in American civilization began with the onset of slavery . . ." (Hernton, 1971). In short, the symbols of sexuality have been unceasingly manipulated to justify oppression and to fan fear and hatred.

Blacks are portrayed not only as oversexed but also as undersexed. ("Indeed," as Du Bois long ago observed, "we black men are continually puzzled by the easy, almost unconscious way in which our detractors change their ground.") Thus Kardiner and Ovesey generalize from their tiny sample that frigidity is "quite frequent" in black women, while sex often seems "relatively unimportant" to the black man. The sex life of blacks of all classes shows "marked deviations from the white stereotypes of hypersexuality." But the harping on hyposexuality also represents a stereotype, and it is reinforced by references to the black man's "uniformly bad relations with females" and "loss in masculinity."

Such approaches, widely influential in the social science literature, have been cogently analyzed by Staples (1971) in his essay on "The Myth of the Impotent Black Male." He writes: "Stereotypes of the black male as psychologically impotent and castrated have been perpetuated not only by social scientists but through the mass media and accepted by both blacks and white alike. Their assault on black masculinity is made *precisely because black males are men;* not because they are impotent, and that is an important distinction to make." It is indeed.

2

It is important to consider how this issue is treated in the psychiatric literature. Does this literature by and large serve to clarify the role of sex in black-white relationships? Does it expose and discredit the racists who encourage the fears and conflicts that sex so easily arouses in many people? Or does it feed, however unintentionally, the stereotypes and distorted emphasis that can only benefit the racists?

In examining the professional literature, we find that much of it is dominated by the view that the vicissitudes and conflicts of sexuality provide the basic motive of racism. The subject is treated mainly in terms of repression, projection, fixation, fetishism, and so forth. Sexual issues are all too often assumed to be the root of racist attitudes and practices.

In the past, this view was stated in baldly simplistic terms. As one psychoanalyst put it, "There probably exists in the unconscious of most, if not all, of the non-African races, a horror of the Negro which can be traced ultimately to sexual jealousy" (Berkeley-Hill, 1924). According to this theory, the black man is hated because he is believed to possess "superior attributes for the act of copulation."

Current formulations are more sophisticated. In the main they emphasize the concept of infantile sexuality as elaborated in psychoanalytic theory. This concept is well expressed in a recent book, *Our Violent Society,* by a prominent psychoanalyst, David Abrahamsen, who asserts that "the Oedipus situation—the old confrontation between father and son—serves as the prototype for all social and political conflicts"

(Abrahamsen, 1970).* When applied to the issue of racism,
this theory postulates that the hatred and anxiety a white
may feel toward blacks are really emotions that are displaced
from early sexual feelings and conflicts regarding the parents.

Not untypical is an article by Gearhart and Schuster
(1971) in *The Archives of General Psychiatry*. They declare
that the white man's attitudes "can be explained in terms of
desexualization of the mother image through idealization and
attributing to the white woman the qualities of chastity, purity,
and disinterest in anything sexual. The sexual, sensual, side
of the mother image is displaced onto the black woman. On
the other hand, the ambivalent rivalrous, fearful attitude toward the father (on the part of the boy) is displaced to the
Negro man, who is then viewed as a hypersexual, violent, rap-
ing (black) beast." As the speculation spins out, it appears
that for a white woman seeking black partners the color difference serves "as a means of expressing the tabooed incest object
as well as the incest barrier. In dreams the black man commonly represents an incestuous object, most often the father."
The authors cite other articles in the psychoanalytical literature with similar formulations, indicating that theirs is not
an isolated view.

Sometimes this theoretical line is developed in simple
terms, uncluttered by other considerations. Some authors,
however, combine a commitment to this viewpoint with a concern for social and historical factors. A notable example of this
trend is Kovel's psychohistory (1970) of white racism.
Though he addresses himself vigorously to a number of social
issues, Kovel still speaks of the "basically sexualized nature

---

* Abrahamsen writes: "Behind race prejudice and violence is a
struggle for power that has been and still is rooted in the Negro's
imagined sexual superiority . . . he [the white man] projects his own
unconsciously directed sexual aggression onto the Negro. . . . Race
violence is thus intimately linked to the *white man's sexual fantasies*.
Pitted against them are the black man's sexual fantasies, inflamed by
his fear of the white man and his longing for revenge upon him. . . ."

of racist psychology," emphasizing the centrality of the "Oedipal situation" and the "repression of instinctual drives."

Whether stated baldly or obliquely, the implications of this theory are clear. If sexual conflicts originating in early infancy are at the root of racial attitudes, then eradication of racism must await the development of a new kind of human being that is somehow free of "Oedipal conflict." With such a perspective, the struggle against political and economic oppression may have some limited usefulness but cannot hope to achieve a fundamental change. Black liberation becomes contingent on emancipation from the id. Such a defeatist attitude is all the more reprehensible when we realize that it is based on a theoretical premise that has never been validated. In the area of racism, the evidence rests on reports of a small number of cases, or even of one case. There have been no systematic studies, with adequate controls, to support the broad speculations about the sexual basis of racism.

Rejection of the theory that sexual conflict is the root cause of racism does not negate the influence of sexual problems on racial attitudes in some people. Far from it. An individual with sexual anxieties may elaborate and exploit racist stereotypes to ameliorate his personal problem. A timid white man may be emboldened to make advances to a black woman because she is, in his mind, "inferior." Or a sexually inhibited white woman may feel that only a black man with his presumed sexual prowess can arouse her. Undoubtedly, in a racist atmosphere the specific form of the psychological problem and ways of solving it may be shaped by racism. But in the instances cited we must assume that if the racial environment were not present, the sexual problems of the individuals would be essentially the same, even though taking different forms. This is a far cry from the theory that would universalize such problems and make them the core of the racist situation.

This distinction has important clinical implications. It is the psychiatrist's responsibility to make clear what the real issue is. The patients' attitudes toward blacks have to be defined, understood, and changed, rather than their attitudes toward their fathers. There is no ground for assuming that changes in attitudes toward the father will necessarily lead to changes in the patient's current relationship to blacks. Evasion of the patient's racist attitudes as expressed in the present situation will hardly help his self-understanding or ability to change.

3

The misuse of the sexual issue to obscure the problem of racist prejudice and oppression is most apparent in relation to the subject of marriage between black and white persons. "Would you want your sister to marry one of them?" is one of the stalest chestnuts in the repertoire of racism. As one student of prejudice observed, "Nowhere else in the world is the question of one's potential brother-in-law considered a fitting retort to the demand for equal pay, decent housing, or the vote" (Goldstein, 1948). This old retort may not be used as openly nowadays, but variations on the same theme are often sounded by people who are convinced that they mean well.

Objections to black-white mating are many times put in terms of the "difficulties" that the partners will face. "I have nothing against it myself, you understand; but it just can't work out because people aren't that developed yet, and this nice couple will encounter overwhelming hostility." Of course, whenever people openly challenge deeply ingrained prejudices, they will meet hostile responses. This is quite evident in the reaction to young people who flout conventional styles of hair and dress. Intermarriage poses an even more intense challenge since it says, in the clearest possible way, through a commitment to joining lives, that the conventional wisdom is being discarded.

Without doubt such a commitment will mean special stresses that will have to be coped with. But there are enough examples of successful interracial marriages to make it clear that such stresses are not necessarily overpowering. As a matter of fact, when a husband and wife meet special problems and stresses—of whatever nature—this can bring them closer if they cope with the problem cooperatively.

The view that such marriages are bound to fail is reinforced by the mass media, which habitually consider a problem-ridden marriage—especially interracial marriage—better copy than a happy, peaceful one. A case in point is that of a national periodical which several years ago ran a picture story on intermarriage. When the article was published, one couple interviewed for this story was surprised to find that they had been left out. They inquired about the reasons for this omission and were told by the magazine that their marriage was not interesting to report because they had no serious problems!

Another rationalization of those who oppose intermarriage is that such marriages are made for neurotic reasons. The marriage may be described as a gesture of defiance (usually of the parents), an act of masochism, a symptom of exhibitionism. It is of interest that emphasis on the neurotic basis of intermarriage is usually directed at the white partner. Presumably it is "understandable" why a black should marry a white, but the reverse "must" be due to some irrational motivation.

Certainly, many black-white marriages may have a neurotic basis. This is inevitable, since a substantial number of all marriages have an unsound basis. It is also true that if a marriage has a neurotic basis and is subject to unusual stresses, the unhealthy aspects of the relationship are likely to become more evident. But this does not validate the assumption that intermarriages are typically unstable. Such sweeping judgments do serious injustice to the healthy, normal individuals who have entered into such marriages, manifesting the strength to withstand social disfavor and the courage to remain faithful to their own feelings. The "neurotic" theory feeds the racist concept that blacks and whites cannot live together on an equal basis.

Another racist argument related to intermarriage is that

the children of such marriages will be insuperably handicapped. One of the most tenacious myths of racism is that persons of "mixed" parentage are more vulnerable to mental disease than those of "pure" stock. Terms like "half-breed," "mongrel," "hybrid," and "mixed-blood," have commonly been used as pejorative tags to explain personality characteristics. Obviously, to call a man a "half-breed" fully accounts for his churlish disposition and unreliable character. The "mixed-blood" suffers from a disharmony and self-division that ultimately generate a mental breakdown. The woebegone and psychologically torn mulatto, a perennial stereotype since the days of slavery, is proof that "amalgamation" of the races can lead only to disaster. In his study of literary stereotypes, Sterling Brown (1969) notes that the fractional theory of mulatto personality finds its *reductio ad absurdum* in Roark Bradford's novel *This Side of Jordan*: "The blade of a razor flashed. . . . Her Negro blood sent it unerringly between the two ribs. Her Indian blood sent it back for an unnecessary second and third slash." To which Brown adds: "It might be hazarded that her Eskimo blood kept her from being chilled with horror."

Such poppycock about the consequences of intermarriage prevailed for generation after generation not only in fiction but also in professional journals. One typical exponent was Dr. C. B. Davenport, a leading zoologist and geneticist, who affirmed that "a hybridized people are a badly put together people and a dissatisfied, restless, ineffective people." Writing in *Archives of Neurology and Psychiatry*, Davenport (1923) asserted that "miscegenation increases the number of new centers of epilepsy," and he wondered "how much of our crime and insanity is due to mental and temperamental friction" resulting from the disharmonious intermixing of races. In his book, *Race Crossing in Jamaica* (1929), Davenport compared white, brown, and black individuals, and found that the browns had a larger number who were "muddled and

wuzzle-headed." What these engaging terms signify was not
made clear, nor was any statistical evidence offered.

But apart from this shoddy superstructure of "research,"
the basic assumption of such studies is of course fallacious.
There are no "pure" races, and there is no reason to think
there ever were. "Mankind always has been, and still is, a
mongrel lot," say two prominent geneticists (Dunn and Dobzhansky, 1952). We are all hybrids and the descendants of
hybrids. Or, as Daniel Defoe wrote,

> "Thus from a mixture of all kinds began
> That heterogeneous thing, an Englishman."

In psychiatry, the concept that "germinal enmity" may
generate mental disease was suggested by Bleuler (1924),
who believed that marked differences in the character predis-
positions of the parents are reflected in a "certain lack of
equilibrium" in the descendants. He added: "The intermin-
gling of races, even those closely related, often has still worse
results although, at least according to superficial observation
of masses, the West Indian Negroes, in whom a white streak
is easily noticed, are a tribe so capable of enjoying life and
so unburdened with any sense of responsibility that one may
well ask whether it is not we who constitute the unsuccessful
variety of humanity." Bleuler had no evidence whatever
(apart from admittedly "superficial observation") for his generalizations about the psychological effects of racial intermin-
gling. This has not prevented others from citing him as an
authority on the subject.

The viewpoint of modern biology has been stated by Ehrlich and Holm (1964). They declare that there is "some reason
to believe that the progeny of parents drawn from two different human populations would be, on the average, more fit in
the sense of the population geneticist than the offspring of
individuals from the same population. There would appear
to be no genetic support either for the encouragement or the

repression of intergroup gene exchange in man. Indeed, the situation of partially differentiated populations with some gene exchange among them has been postulated to be the ideal state for further evolution."

Yet the word "miscegenation," with its negative overtones, is still widely used to describe intergroup mating. The acceptance of this term is a graphic example of how racist ideas achieve uncritical circulation. The word "miscegenation" (literally, a mixture of races) does not have an authentic origin in science. It was actually invented by two New York newspapermen as part of a provocative political hoax designed to discredit Abraham Lincoln and the antislavery forces in the election campaign of 1864. They published an anonymous booklet, titled *Miscegenation: The Theory of the Blending of the Races,* purporting to be written by Abolitionists who advocated systematic race-mixing as the cure-all for the nation's problems (Kaplan, 1949; Wood, 1968). The word was picked up by the racists as a term of opprobrium and its unthinking use today represents a victory for the Copperheads who concocted it.*

---

* In *An American Dilemma,* Myrdal (1944) observes: "Miscegenation is mainly an American term and is in America almost always used to denote only relations between Negroes and whites. Although it literally implies only mixture of genes between members of different races, it has acquired a definite emotional connotation. We use it in its literal sense—without implying necessarily that it is undesirable—as a convenient synonym of amalgamation." But how can a term with such a "definite emotional connotation" be convenient to use in a scientific work that seeks to shed light on the emotional subject of racism in America? Besides, the word did not simply "acquire" this connotation" but originated with it.

8

The "Sickness" of
White Racism

"The habit of considering racism as a mental quirk, as a psychological flaw, must be abandoned."

FRANTZ FANON (1967)

I

IN EXPLAINING the origin and meaning of racism, it has become ritualistic to invoke psychiatric concepts. The roots of prejudice are sought in the "sick personality" or the "sick white psyche." Many authors speak of frustration-aggression, projection, anxiety, and guilt. Such terms suggest that racism necessarily reflects psychopathology. It is often argued that a mentally normal person cannot be a racist, and that a racist cannot be a mentally normal person. Just as Hitler was characterized as a madman and the Germans as a paranoid nation, so the white racists in American society are described in terms of psychological aberrations.

This equation between racism and mental illness is a tempting one to make. So distorted are the racist's values that it seems natural to associate them with psychological disturbance. But the "sickness" metaphor does not constitute a diagnosis. Racism, unfortunately, is not the monopoly of a single type of personality structure. All kinds of people can be and are racists: normal and abnormal, paranoid and non-paranoid, aggressive and passive, domineering and submissive. Mental illness cannot be equated with socially offensive attitudes and practices.

Some people feel that to label racists as "sick" is the ultimate indictment. On the contrary, it is the assumption that racists are all disturbed persons that lets them off the hook. A mentally ill individual cannot be held fully accountable for his behavior. The full horror of systematic prejudice can be grasped only if it is seen as a characteristic of persons who are not deranged. When we view the racist as a creature driven by blind and irresistible psychodynamic forces, we cushion his crime. The massacres at Auschwitz or Mylai are all the more horrible because they were perpetrated by men who were not mental cases.

In our society, racist acts and attitudes are so institutionalized that they can be indulged in as a matter of course by persons who are not pathological. This view agrees with that developed by Daniels and Kitano in their illuminating book on *American Racism* (1970). They write: "We feel that the consistent attacks on various social groups are impossible to explain solely from the 'sick personality' approach, unless one is willing to assume the existence of an extremely large number of such people, past, present, and possibly in the future." Racist attitudes in America can hardly be viewed as idiosyncratic. They are all too "normal." The millions who participate in discriminatory practices exhibit wide variations in regard to such categories as frustration, authoritarianism, intolerance of ambiguity, "Oedipal conflicts" and other presumed explanations of the racist personality.*

At the same time, it is true that certain social values can

---

* Some sociologists recognize that "It is probable that the search for the determinants of prejudice and discrimination in attitudinal sets, personality structure, or role-specific behavior has inhibited the development of a social structural perspective on race relations in American sociology" (Metzger, 1971).

feed and reinforce pathological trends in an individual. The paranoid type may readily fasten his fears of persecution on the "aggressive" Jew or the "primitive" black, while using the myth of racial superiority to bolster his fantasies of grandeur. For those white people who are sadists, who need to project their sexual fantasies on to others, or who must compensate for feelings of inadequacy by degrading others, American society long ago furnished an approved target by declaring open season on blacks. "Nobody was more vulnerable to the 'projection of evil' or psychological exploitation than the black man," observes Comer (1969). The psychological exploitation has been as real as the economic exploitation of black people throughout American history.

Psychological exploitation of the black is so extensive that psychiatrists and psychologists constantly encounter its manifestations in white patients. Its expression may be crude and overt, or subtle and disguised. In their dreams, white patients commonly use the Negro as a symbol of a person to be degraded or to be feared (not as an authority figure but as a "primitive" threat). Society has encouraged such suppressions. As Comer notes, "Racism is a low-level defense and adjustment mechanism utilized by groups to deal with psychological and social insecurities similar to the manner in which individuals utilize psychic defenses and adjustment mechanisms to deal with anxiety. . . . A given society may promote and reward racism to enable members of the group in control to obtain a sense of personal adequacy and security at the expense of the group with less control."

2

Most psychiatric theorists who have attempted to explain racism have done so in psychodynamic terms. Viewing racism as presumably a psychological phenomenon, they have sought a psychological cause within the framework of prevailing psychiatric theory. If white racism manifests itself in the behavior, language, and attitudes of individuals, then its roots must presumably lie in instinctual drives, infantile stages of psychological development, or specific types of personality structure.

For example, one often encounters in the psychoanalytic literature the thesis that racist violence directed against blacks has its origin in the infantile unconscious. Typical of this approach is a discussion by Sterba (1947) of race riots in Detroit. The author traces the irrationality of anti-Negro outbursts to infantile tendencies. The first is sibling jealousy, which generates in the older child feelings of hatred and disgust for the younger child. "The hostility is repressed, but preserved in the unconscious, and then directed against the Negroes as a substitute object. In this respect the Negroes signify younger siblings." The white racist's fear of dethronement "mirrors exactly" the older child's attitude toward his sibling rivals.

The second cause of anti-black violence postulated by Sterba derives from the nuclear psychoanalytic concept of the Oedipus complex. "Psychologically," he maintains, "Negro race riots are violent outbreaks of infantile father hatred." This has its origins in the South, where many white children are brought up by a "mammy" to whom they often develop feelings like those toward a mother. "Due to the development of the oedipus complex, the male Negro is then naturally brought into the position of the hated father." In a lynching, the rebellious sons unite against the hated father to castrate and kill him.

This mode of explanation reduces the event to an exercise in psychodynamic abstractions. The persons taking part in the violence appear as mythic symbols that might as well represent the bloody happenings in ancient Troy as the confrontation in Detroit. We are not told how many of the white rioters never had a "mammy" and so did not have this oedipal spur to destroy black men. Nor do we learn how many of the white racists were themselves younger siblings or came from families where they were the only child. The formula derives from the mechanical application of an *a priori* theory rather than a painstaking study of the facts.

Another psychoanalytic theory stresses "the anal components of white hostility and aggression toward the Negro" (Hamilton, 1964). This concept was used to explain the "overreaction" of a white woman when she learned that blacks were planning to buy a house on her street in Ann Arbor, Michigan. The woman had been told by a realtor that if the blacks moved in, her property would be devalued by $2,000. But the threat of a money loss presumably represented something deeper: "Freud first commented on the function of money as a sublimation of the wish to play with feces." In the housing dispute, the white woman and her family "were faced with a strengthening of the forbidden instinctual wish to play with feces. . . ." The author's identification of "anal dynamics in determining the reaction of white persons to integrated housing" conjures up quite an image of anal fixation in white suburbia.

A variant of the Freudian postulate is the "frustration-aggression" hypothesis. As developed by John Dollard and his associates (1939), this theory assumes that aggression is always a consequence of frustration. The object of the aggression may be "direct"; that is, the same as the frustrating agent. But the aggression may also be "displaced" onto a scapegoat; that is, the frustration is taken out on an available rather than a logical object. The process is described as usually unconscious. Rationalizations cover up the real reasons for the "displaced" aggression.

Race animosity is cited as a specific illustration of the relation between frustration and aggression. "For, according to the hypothesis, the existence of a social prejudice against a group of people is evidence, first, that those who have the prejudice have been frustrated and, secondly that they are expressing their aggression or part of it in fairly uniform fashion" (Dollard *et al.*, 1939). The situation of blacks in the United States was described in terms of this hypothesis by Dollard in *Caste and Class in a Southern Town* (1937). According to this view, the anti-black riots that took place in Chicago and East St. Louis after World War I were examples of direct aggression, since the rioters identified blacks moving into their communities as the cause of their frustration. Often, however, aggression is displaced onto blacks with whom the racist has had no contact.

The "scapegoat" hypothesis, while undoubtedly based on a truth, does not offer a master key for understanding the nature of prejudice. As Allport (1954) observed in his classic study of prejudice, the theory "fails to supply the many differentials needed: why some people respond to frustration in an aggressive manner; why some types of frustration are more likely to induce displacements upon out-groups; why some people persist in displacement in spite of its complete failure as a mode of adaptation; or why, on the other hand, some people hold the displacement tendency in check, and never allow it to affect their ethnic attitudes." The concept of aggression as an undifferentiated devouring force is too global, covering too many different kinds of acts carried out for different kinds of reasons and with different kinds of consequences.

Moreover, Dollard's theory, like other psychodynamic formulations, assumes that "the unconscious" plays a major part in racist attitudes, though no convincing evidence is offered to support this view. Dollard himself was on firmer ground when he identified three specific "gains"—economic, sexual, and prestige—accruing to middle-class whites in his Southern town as a result of black oppression. The whites are well aware of these gains, and pursue them quite consciously and deliberately. To stress the "unconscious" component of racist aggression is to relieve the racist of full responsibility for his behavior.*

---

* This absolution for the racist can go so far as to claim that prejudice may contribute to the psychological health of the individual and have beneficial social effects. Thus, Bird (1957) in the *Journal of the American Psychoanalytic Association* asserted that prejudice can be an ego defense mechanism for dealing with unconscious ag-

3

Another influential view regarding the psychology of prejudice centers on "the authoritarian personality." As formulated by Adorno and his colleagues (1950), this concept assumes that there is a basic type of prejudiced personality in which a syndrome of "authoritarian" traits can be identified. These traits include extreme deference to superior authority, close conformity to group norms, tendency to manipulate people as objects, rigidity of thought processes, lack of self-insight, and excessive sense of one's own moral rightness. The authoritarian personality craves definiteness; it cannot tolerate ambiguity. Everything is either good or evil, right or wrong, with no shadings or contradictions, no possibility of compromise or compassion. It is postulated that such a personality derives from a childhood in which parental discipline has been severe, or the parent has been rejecting and manipulative. The child becomes submissive, though strong feelings of hostility may be aroused against the parents and other authority figures. Since such hostility must often be repressed out of fear of punishment, the feelings are displaced toward safer targets. These include minority groups and others with inferior status.

In a descriptive sense, there may be much validity to this formulation of a certain constellation of personality attributes for which the term "authoritarian" may be quite apt. It is also not unlikely that individuals with this personality pattern may show more extreme forms of racism as well as other forms of bigotry (religious, anti-foreign, etc.). Such a personality type may gravitate more than others toward ideologies that preach

---

gressive impulses, and that "According to this formulation, prejudice is seen to be one of the peculiar but not uncommon mental mechanisms which, although thoroughly objectionable in its effect, yet is not without a positive measure of value for the individual and in a broad way for society as a whole." It is a sad commentary that this article has been cited approvingly by other psychoanalysts and has not received, so far as we know, any refutation in the psychoanalytic literature. Fourteen years later Bird's thesis was challenged in the general psychiatric literature by a black psychiatrist (Robinson, 1971).

hatred and contempt for groups perceived as "alien." However, the fact that one may find more "authoritarians" among the extreme racists does not prove that this psychological constellation produces the racist attitudes. Both the personality type and the racism may be produced by some other cause; or they may be produced independently, but then become interactive phenomena, one reinforcing the other.

The data of the Adorno study and similar investigations are not sufficient to resolve the question. Moreover, even if a relation were established between the authoritarian personality and racism, this would not explain the prevalence of racism among persons representing many other kinds of personality structure.

In the years since the Dollard and Adorno studies were published, it has become increasingly clear that the profound social dimensions of white racism cannot be comprehended through a psychogenetic explanation. This awareness is reflected in the attempts of some psychiatrists to combine their commitment to psychoanalytic theory with a serious sociohistorical analysis of the causes of white racism. A notable example is the book *White Racism: A Psychohistory* (1970) by Dr. Joel Kovel of the Albert Einstein College of Medicine. In this ambitious effort to integrate Freudian theory and social analysis, Kovel seeks to show that racism is both "a set of beliefs whose structure arises from the deepest levels of our lives" and "the product of the historical unfolding of Western culture."

In fact, however, the author repeatedly falls back on classical psychoanalytic theory to explain the basic causes of racism. Thus, in the same vein as Sterba a quarter-century earlier, Kovel asserts that "Only the theory of the Oedipus complex—enlarged into a cultural apparatus that defines and binds real roles even as it apportions fantasies amongst the players of these roles—will account for this variety of phenomena." The repression of the black man in the South is explained in terms of the white male's "castrating the father, as he once wished to do, and also identifying with the father by castrating the son, as he once feared for himself. All that he has to do to maintain this delectable position is to structure his society so that he directly dominates black men." If white racism is rooted in such infantile instinctual forces, ubiquitous and overpowering, it is no wonder that Kovel takes a basically pessimistic view of the possibilities for change.

4

Such pessimism about the possibility of change in social attitudes and group behavior flows logically from the belief that they are rooted in instinctual life. One is reminded of the famous exchange of letters between Freud and Einstein on the subject of preventing war. In opposition to Einstein, Freud took the view that war is the expression of an unchangeable death instinct and is therefore inevitable. While world events, unfortunately, have yet to refute Freud's gloomy prediction, his theory does not explain why some countries go to war repeatedly and others remain at peace for many generations and even centuries.

To give primacy to social causes does not mean that the psychological expressions of racism are accidental or superficial. These manifestations may have deep roots in personality. They may profoundly affect an individual's thinking and behavior. They nevertheless remain essentially the consequences, not the causes of racism.

It may be objected that it is mechanical and simplistic to make a categorical distinction between cause and effect as against a dynamic consideration of interactive phenomena. There is indeed continuous interaction. The psychological consequences reinforce the social institutions of racism. But identification of cause is essential for a strategy of change. If the basic causes are social, then the primary emphasis must be on changing social institutions, such as the elimination of inequalities of civil rights, education, and job opportunity. If the basic causes are psychological, we would have to be concerned primarily with such issues as mother-child relationships, child-care practices, and sibling rivalry.

To be sure, prejudice is not automatically and immediately eliminated by changes in social institutions. This persistence is especially marked in the case of race prejudice, "in which the traditionally transmitted antipathies often provide the central core around which there gather other supporting antipathies constituting together an emotional system difficult to eradicate" (Ginsberg, 1964). People cling to ideas and behavior that are clearly not only in conflict with reality and developing knowledge, but are also destructive to themselves. It would be the height of naivete to expect that the social changes required to eliminate racism can be achieved without difficult and prolonged struggle. But it would be utter defeatism to conclude that resistance to change reflects the operation of some fixed psychic force, whether this be labelled original sin, collective unconscious, aggression, territoriality, or death instinct.

9

Pitfalls of Epidemiology

I

IN EVERY BRANCH of medicine, one of the basic tools for furthering knowledge is epidemiology, the study of the frequency and distribution of disease in human populations. Detection of illness patterns according to age, occupation, residence, or socioeconomic group can yield valuable clues to the cause and control of disease. A classic instance occurred during an outbreak of cholera in London over 100 years ago. By studying the distribution of cases, Dr. John Snow deduced that the epidemic had its source in a single contaminated water pump. In our own day, epidemiological studies identified the link between cigarette smoking and lung cancer.

In psychiatry, too, the study of disease rates and patterns plays an important role. Such research can be used to determine which sectors of a population are under greatest stress. The observation that a particular group has a greater incidence of schizophrenia or depression may put one on the track of some organic or social factor that is more prevalent in this group than in the general population. The well-known work of Hollingshead and Redlich (1958) on *Social Class and Mental Illness*, based on a study of the New Haven community, reported a high prevalence of serious mental disorder in the most disadvantaged economic group, and documented the class bias in treatment and rehabilitation opportunities. Current investigations into the familial incidence of schizophrenia may help clarify the comparative role of environmental and genetic factors in this disorder.

A major area of epidemiological study in psychiatry is the comparison of mental illness rates among blacks and whites. The range of such investigations has been impressively wide. Ethnic differences in the incidence of mental disease have been surveyed in New York (Malzberg, 1959), in Chicago (Faris and Dunham, 1939), in Baltimore (Klee, 1967), and many other centers. The findings have often been imprecise and contradictory. A North Carolina study (Vitols, 1963) found a "considerably higher incidence" of hallucinations in black than in white schizophrenics. A Florida study (Simon, 1965) reported a "lower incidence" of involutional psychosis among black women than among white women, though there was no difference between black men and white men. An Ohio study of first admissions to state mental hospitals found that "Negroes have exceedingly higher rates of mental illness than do whites," but it was also noted that admission rates were higher among the poor, both black and white, suggesting that "the low status of the Negro rather than some biological or genetic difference due to 'race' accounted for the disproportionate figures." An Illinois study of first admissions to state mental hospitals revealed "no greater incidence of psychosis in Negroes than whites" (McLean, 1949). And an exhaustive Texas study indicated lower rates of mental illness among blacks (Jaco, 1960).

As one reviews the literature comparing mental disease patterns in the black and white populations, it becomes plain that most investigators have jumped to sweeping generalizations on the basis of skimpy evidence. All too often these speculations have been used to reinforce racist concepts. And this has occurred whether it was concluded that black people have more mental illness or less mental illness than whites. True, the more widespread notion among social scientists, as Fischer (1969) documents in a fine review, is the "myth, simply stated, that Negroes have more mental illness than whites" and this has bolstered the postulate of inferiority. But the thesis that blacks are *less* susceptible to mental illness, particularly depression and psychoneurosis, has also been advanced as part of the argument that blacks are "less sensitive" or "less complicated" than white people. In short, you're damned if you're ill, and you're damned if you aren't—and this is so whether the explanation offered is genetic or sociological, and whether statistics are ostentatiously employed or the assertion is nakedly verbal.

2

The misuse of epidemiology to suggest that freedom unhinges the black man's mind dates back to the Census of 1840, as we have already noted. This thesis was echoed during the Reconstruction and post-Reconstruction periods.* It was recently revived by some psychiatrists who asserted that the civil rights movement and its successes lead to an increased rate of mental illness among blacks. In this view, gains in civil rights are a mixed blessing. By unsettling a structured way of life in which group roles are clearly defined, desegregation is "anxiety-producing." The black man, assailed by the ambiguities of cultural change, succumbs to severe emotional disorders.

This theory was bluntly formulated in a paper read at the American Psychiatric Association meeting in 1956 by D. C. Wilson, chairman of the Psychiatry Department of the Uni-

---

* In 1903, the distinguished American psychiatrist William Alanson White asserted that "the percentage of colored insane increases rapidly as we leave the natural home of the negro and go in any direction. In other words, as soon as the negro goes north and enters into active competition with the white, who is mentally his superior, he succumbs in the unequal struggle." The echoes reverberate in the influential *Textbook of Psychiatry* by Eugen Bleuler (1924). This eminent Swiss psychiatrist wrote that "in America it was discovered that the negroes, who as slaves had no percentage of insanity worth mentioning, become insane in greater numbers the more they approach the manner of living of the whites. . . ." Karl Jaspers also cites this alleged fact in his *General Psychopathology* (1963), but this German psychiatrist more cautiously adds, "Any plausible interpretation seems impossible in view of the little known material and the impossibility of testing it critically."

versity of Virginia. The paper, which was widely quoted in the general press, cited a "tremendous increase" in the admission rate of black patients to state hospitals in Virginia between 1914 and 1954. The rise was reported to be especially marked during the last ten years of the period under study, and it was concluded that "there is more mental illness among the Negroes of Virginia than among the whites" (Wilson and Lantz, 1957). To explain this disparity, the report emphasized the harmful impact of the loss of "definite status" once enjoyed by the blacks.

"From 1877 to 1915," observed Wilson and his co-author Lantz, "the Negro was segregated under the definite concept that he was an inferior being, lived in a culture of his own, and was supposed to know his place, which though respected, was nevertheless subservient to the white. The Negro was supposed to be very happy, very religious, and free from the anxieties that troubled the whites. . . . Forty years ago the Negro and white family lived across the street from each other. The children played together and the adult Negroes worked in the home or on the farm. The Negro had a definite status." But now, despite legal victories and higher income, he is uneasy because he has lost his clear-cut place and is "constantly stirred up" by the "propaganda of his leaders, by the Communists and by those politicians who would use this power." His new position is being imposed from outside, and "Cultural changes which are forced on a people against their will . . . have been found by the experts of the UN to produce major disturbances of mental health."

As for blacks who migrated to the North, their rate of mental illness is even higher, the authors maintain. And again the explanation is not far to seek in the realm of speculation: "The probabilities are that the more unstable members of the race migrated."

Aside from its obvious echoes of antebellum mythology, the Wilson-Lantz paper is worth examining because it exemplifies so clearly the multiple pitfalls of epidemiology. The paper

126   RACISM AND PSYCHIATRY

has been searchingly reviewed by Benjamin Pasamanick
(1963, 1964), a leading authority on psychiatric epidemiology.
To begin with, Pasamanick challenges the validity of the statistical findings that mental disease is more prevalent among
blacks than whites. State hospital rates cannot be assumed to
give an accurate picture of the incidence or prevalence of disease. White patients are admitted to private facilities that are
unavailable to black patients. In Virginia, the reported difference between admissions of blacks and whites diminishes
sharply (from a ratio of 2.5:1 to 1.3:1) if data are included
from other facilities as well as state hospitals.*

In the Wilson-Lantz study, rates of institutionalization for
mental deficiency and alcoholism were found to be higher for
whites than for black persons. "A naive observer," comments
Pasamanick, "might conclude that the task of segregating the
Negroes in Virginia is so difficult and frustrating that it produces mental deficiency and alcoholism. What is probably more
likely is that facilities for mental deficiency, as well as demands for institutionalization, are greater among whites, and
that the Negro alcoholic is committed to jail rather than the
hospital."

Pasamanick also points out that the misuse of mental hospital data has a long history affecting not only blacks but also
the foreign-born. Faulty interpretations of crude rates for hospitalized psychotics were widely used for many years to slan-
der Irish Catholics and then Southern European and Eastern
European immigrants.**

---

* And as Pettigrew (1964) points out, "Once committed, Negro
lower-class patients, like lower-class patients in general, are less likely
to receive advanced therapy; indeed, they may well receive only
custodial care and thus be assigned to lengthy institutionalization."
This is one of several factors operating to "elevate spuriously both
the incidence and prevalence mental illness rates of Negroes, since
they amplify the number of Negroes institutionalized without necessarily representing an actual increase in the amount of mental illness."
** In the 1850's, prejudice against poor Irish immigrants was mir-
rored in the reports of mental asylum superintendents. They com-
plained that these immigrants were filling up the asylums because
they were unable to adapt to the more civilized American way of life,

The biometrics branch of the National Institute of Mental Health has repeatedly cautioned against making comparisons between whites and Negroes based on data drawn from hospitals in different areas of the country. Admission rates are influenced by the age distribution of state populations, the number of beds available, legal and administrative procedures, distance of hospitals from the patients' homes. Not only admission rates but also the total number of patients in mental hospitals will depend on a variety of factors. These include the extent to which psychotropic drugs are used, the introduction of hospital policies favoring earlier discharge, the availability of outpatient and community facilities. Clearly such questions must be taken into account in epidemiological studies. Yet simplistic thinking continues in this sphere, particularly in the assumption that black patients have access to the same range of facilities and treatment modalities as do white patients.

Another pitfall of epidemiology is the problem of defining mental illness in general and of identifying specific disorders. Despite all efforts of the American Psychiatric Association to achieve a consensus in its *Diagnostic and Statistical Manual,* psychiatrists do not see eye-to-eye on the classification of behavioral disturbance. Since different investigators use different criteria, one psychiatrist may end up diagnosing more cases as schizophrenia while another designates more cases as psychoneurotic. In addition, there are changing fashions in psychiatric diagnosis as in general medical diagnosis. This may partly explain the Wilson-Lantz finding of an increase of schizophrenia among blacks in Virginia. As the schizophrenia rate

could not grasp "our language," huddled in the hovels and filth of overcrowded cities, and preferred "the excitement or solace of rum or tobacco to the quiet intelligent influences of well-ordered houses," in the words of the superintendent of the State Lunatic Asylum at Worcester, Mass. This institution segregated its Irish patients, and leading New England psychiatrists advocated separate asylums for native and foreign born patients on the theory that the mental illness of the refined natives would be worsened if they continued to be housed with the "coarse, filthy, impulsive" foreigners (Dain, 1964).

rose, there was a corresponding decline in manic depressive psychoses. Evidently, as Pasamanick notes, over the years there was a shift in the style of diagnosis rather than in the incidence of schizophrenia.

A further problem is that a white psychiatrist may attach different pathological significance to the same symptom or behavioral deviation in a black patient and a white patient. In part this may be due to a class slant, inasmuch as a number of studies have indicated that upper-class persons are more likely than lower-class persons to be diagnosed as psychoneurotic. Beyond this, there seems to be a greater tendency to tag certain symptoms as neurotic when they appear in white patients and as due to psychosis or psychopathic personality when they appear in black patients (Gross, 1969). Such differential judgments may even be crudely exploited for racist purposes as in the formulation of a New Orleans psychiatrist who reported that "it is our impression that for several reasons neuroticism is likely to be less frequent among Negroes than among white subjects, probably because of the differences in the cultural and civilization level of the two races" (Wexberg, 1941).*

2

The psychiatric literature has also devoted much attention to the comparative rates of depression in black and white patients. It has been repeatedly asserted that depression is rarely found among blacks (Babcock, 1895; O'Malley, 1914; Bevis, 1921; Prange and Vitols, 1962). In the earlier studies this finding was linked to the traditional stereotype of the "happy-

---

* Pettigrew (1964) observes: "If group data on psychosis are difficult to decipher, group data on neurosis are even more confusing. Most of these less serious mental abnormalities do not require institutionalization; particularly among lower-status Negroes, neurotic symptoms may often be ignored." Reported higher rates of first admissions to state hospitals for neurosis "may merely reflect that only incapacitated Negroes are accepted. In addition, many neurotics receive treatment from private sources, and for economic reasons these individuals are predominantly white."

go-lucky" Negro, blessed by nature with high spirits and unburdened by a sense of responsibility. "Naturally," one psychiatrist asserted, "most of the race are care-free, live in the
'here and now' with a limited capacity to recall or profit by
experiences of the past. Sadness and depression have little part
in his psychological makeup" (Bevis, 1921). More recently,
the contention that black people are depression-proof has been
couched in more sophisticated forms.

Thus two North Carolina psychiatrists (Prange and Vitols,
1962) adopt the premise of psychodynamic theory that depression is usually precipitated by the experience of a loss that
typically involves prestige, esteem, real goods, or an ambiva-
lently loved person. Since the southern Negro "has less to lose
and is less apt to lose it," he is less vulnerable to depression.
As defenses against loss, he has attitudes of stoicism and subtle
defiance, religion, an extended family relationship; he can
also "projectively" locate the source of misfortune outside
himself, the opposite of the "introjective," self-blaming mechanism basic to depression. Prange and Vitols conclude: "Depression was once known as the English malady; in the United
States it could be called the white man's malady. We ask the
indulgence of a prediction: as the Negro comes to share more
fully the white man's culture, he will also share his malady."

The evidence produced by Prange and Vitols for the rarity
of depression among blacks is meager. It is based on a comparison of first admissions to the one public facility for mentally ill blacks in North Carolina and two other state hospitals.
Only 1 percent of the blacks as against 4.3 percent of the
whites were diagnosed as having psychotic-depressive reactions. But the authors acknowledge that important questions
affecting selection for hospitalization could not be answered:
"For example, in the South is depression considered an adequate reason to hospitalize a Negro? Do depressed Negroes
seek and find medical care?" And one may add other pertinent
queries: Does the fact that there was only one mental facility
for blacks in the entire state, with consequent difficulty of

access, have a bearing? Were the same diagnostic criteria employed in the black facility and the other hospitals?

The hazards of generalizing about this issue are under-
scored by a more objective investigation, also conducted in
North Carolina, that produced opposite findings. In a longitudinal study of elderly persons residing in the Piedmont area
of the state, two Duke University psychiatrists (Dovenmuehle
and McGough, 1965) tested the hypothesis that the incidence
of depressive experience would be higher among the white subjects than among the blacks. The hypothesis could not be sub-
stantiated. On the contrary, "the findings of this study would
lead to the conclusion that Negroes and lower social class
subjects experience more disabling depression than their white
and higher class cohorts."

The investigators suggest that "hypotheses about racial
and cultural differences in mental illness patterns based on
hospital admission rates do not hold up when applied to community populations." Evidence of differences between racial
groups in the incidence of *treated* depressive syndromes "does
not necessarily imply that these differences are the direct result
of constitution, culture, personality, or family patterns and
child rearing practices." Many black persons with depression
do not present themselves at hospitals, and when they do they
may not be recognized as depressive by hospital physicians.
"What in effect happens is the cultural determinants of a given
group of patients determine the sample in which they are
found. For example, in Vitols' report [discussed above] the
hospital sampled is a great distance from the homes of many
of its patients and is traditionally dreaded and sometimes
avoided by patients who might otherwise utilize it. Depressed
patients can more easily avoid hospitalization than excited
patients or schizophrenics."

While accepting the psychodynamic postulate that links
depression to loss of valued human ties, personal possessions,
or prestige, these investigators contradict the conclusion of
Prange and Vitols that blacks are less depressed because they

have less to lose. Instead, they note that "The aged, the Negro, and the lower social class have been found to suffer more losses with respect to income, access to prestigeful occupation, and health than younger, white and upper class groups. In this regard, age, race, and social class may influence the frequency of precipitating factors in depression, serving as active predisposing factors."

Apart from the question of incidence, the psychiatric literature has also contrasted the specific character of depressions among blacks and whites. It is usually asserted that somatic complaints are likely to predominate in blacks, while feelings of guilt and suicidal trends are more evident in whites. The reported difference has been attributed to variations in family structure, child rearing practices, and cultural norms. "While these formulations have gained moderate acceptance in the folklore of social psychiatry, statistical and empirical support has been meager," reports a group of Yale psychiatrists (Tonks *et al.*, 1970). After systematically comparing black and white patients in several New Haven mental health facilities, the psychiatrists concluded that "the differences between the two groups that one might have expected, based on statements from the literature, were conspicuous only by their absence."

Related to the issue of depression is that of suicide, which occurs most frequently, though not exclusively, in depressed individuals. Studies of suicides among blacks have developed, in the main, only recently. In general they have been free of the racist stereotypes that characterized so many of the earlier studies of depression. A number of discussions have attempted to explain the lower national suicide rates that have been reported for blacks by the National Center for Health Statistics. After middle age, the rates for suicide among black males decline rather than continuing to rise steeply as do rates for whites. Clark (1965) notes that the suicide rate in Harlem is lower than the New York City average (8.2 per 100,000 population as against the city rate of 9.7). In the South, the apparent discrepancy in suicide rates has given rise to an astonishing dogma. "Some veteran southern physicians," we are told, "who have had extensive experience treating Negroes consider a serious suicidal attempt to be *prima facie* evidence of white ancestry" (Prange and Vitols, 1962).

The most ambitious study of this problem has been done by Herbert Hendin, a psychiatrist who had previously investigated suicide in Scandinavia. In his *Black Suicide* (1969), Hendin argues that the focus on the high frequency of suicide among older whites led to the misconception that suicide is a "white" problem. This focus has obscured the fact that "among young adults of both sexes, particularly in urban areas, it is actually more of a black problem." In New York, for example, the rate of suicide among black men between the ages of 20 and 25 is twice as high as among white men in the same age group.

Using psychoanalytic interviewing techniques, Hendin studied 25 black patients who made suicide attempts. "These suicidal patients do more than tell us about black suicide," he reports. "They dramatize the general pressures and conflicts of Negro life; they hold an enlarged mirror up to the frustration and anger of the black ghetto. Unfortunately their problems vary only in degree from those of larger masses of urban blacks on the bottom of the social scale." Hendin repeats the standard generalization that black family life is characterized by maternal rejection, paternal brutality, and crippled self-esteem. Essentially he echoes Kardiner and Ovesey's *The Mark of Oppression,* which Hendin feels "provides the best analysis of the ways in which racial oppression disrupts the black family and helps to perpetuate the black person's problems"—a commentary on how attractive this thesis continues to be for many psychiatrists in spite of its basic distortions.

In answer to those blacks who "resent studies that emphasize this role of the black family," Hendin declares that "to deny psychological facts, however, no matter how well-intentioned the political motive, results only in propaganda." This appeal to scientific objectivity is a red herring. The issue is not "denial" of psychological facts, but rather a demand that the conclusions be based on adequate data. It would not be considered valid procedure to form sweeping judgments about white family life from a study of 25 white suicidal patients. Conclusions about the black family based on such a sample are equally open to question. Hendin has made a contribution by challenging the conventional assumption that suicide is a "white" problem. But in attempting to account for black suicide he simplistically infers group pathology from individual pathology.*

4

A number of studies have investigated the relationship between mental disorder and the migration of blacks from South to North. Here too the reported findings have been contradictory. Malzberg and Lee (1956) found that black persons who moved to New York State from the South had higher rates of mental disorder than blacks born in that state. But an attempt to replicate this study in Pennsylvania yielded different results. Parker and Kleiner (1966) found that rates of first admissions to state hospitals were significantly higher among blacks born in Pennsylvania than among migrants. Their findings also contradicted the prevailing hypothesis of "culture shock," according to which newcomers entering an unaccustomed social environment may experience such psychological difficulties as value conflicts, role discrimination, and social disorientation. Blacks moving to Philadelphia from other urban areas had higher rates than those coming from rural areas even though the latter were presumably more vulnerable to "culture shock." Moreover, illness rates for migrants living

---

* Similar questions are raised in a review of Hendin's book in the *American Journal of Psychiatry* by Dr. Charles B. Wilkinson (1970), who notes: "Although the author refers to the cohort as a small one, through inference by indicating it to be a cross sample of the black ghetto he presents it as a representative cohort of the total black segregated population . . . the diversity evident in black persons and families has been missed."

in the city less than five years were lower for those living there longer (Kleiner and Parker, 1969). The investigators speculate that the higher mental illness rates among blacks living longer in the North might be due to their relatively higher levels of social mobility and goal-striving behavior as well as their "weak or ambivalent attitudes toward their Negro group membership."

In reviewing epidemiological studies of the mental health of blacks, then, the contradictory findings and tenuous explanations should give pause to anyone inclined to rush toward definitive conclusions. The descriptive data are often spotty and subjective, their interpretation arbitrary. Hypotheses that escape rigorous testing nevertheless pass as truths. The persons under study are seldom a representative sample of the population. "The Negro is over-diagnosed in some categories, under-diagnosed in others, given selective treatment and perhaps none at all if a presenting symptom is believed to be a 'cultural characteristic' " (Gullattee, 1969).

Above all, the uncritical worship of statistics can be especially damaging here. Bald figures in themselves do not authenticate a proposition. The figures may be implicitly biased in favor of the group considered normal, so that statistical deviations from the model are assumed to be behavioral deviations. And even if the statistical finding is free of bias and can be accepted as accurate, this is still only the beginning of investigation, not the end point, in a field where so many complex variables interact and can influence the results. It is a tricky matter to tease out the *functional* significance of findings regarded as "statistically significant." Statistics express correlations, but one must not assume that causal relationships can be deduced from such correlations. The fact that more mental illness is found among the poor does not clearly establish the etiological significance of social class variables. Nor do statistical findings about the prevalence of mental illness among blacks establish that the explanation lies in the condition of being black.

10

The Black Patient: Separate and Unequal

I

RACIST PRECONCEPTIONS may distort the psychiatric treatment process at every stage. Such ideas influence the criteria for patient acceptance, availability of facilities, form and length of therapy, nature of the patient-therapist relationship, therapeutic goals, and judgment of outcome.

Unequal opportunities for treatment are apparent in every type of practice—office, clinic, and hospital. All too many psychiatrists, whether deliberately or unwittingly, do not meet their professional obligation to treat black patients. Differences in access to treatment are facts of life that are as palpable as differences in access to good housing, schools, and jobs.

This is most obvious in individual psychotherapy. A study by the American Psychoanalytic Association indicated that 99% of the 10,000 patients under treatment by 800 members of the association were white (Hamburg, 1967). Other surveys have been unable to detect even this minute fraction of black patients. Representative groups of analysts treat white patients only, even though these analysts practice in areas that include large black populations (Siegel, 1962; Weintraub and Aronson, 1968). The high financial cost of psychoanalysis is no doubt a major reason for the virtual exclusion of blacks from

135

private therapy. There is no evidence, however, that the analysts surveyed make any effort to overcome the *de facto* discrimination by reducing fees for poor patients, in keeping with
an honorable medical tradition.

But the fee barrier is only part of the story. Actually,
racial selection of patients for individual treatment is prac-
ticed in settings where ability to pay for services is presumably
not the overriding issue—for example, in training programs
for psychiatric residents. In a remarkable report, five black
psychiatrists (Jones *et al.*, 1970) have described their experience as residents in three predominantly white, psycho-
analytically oriented training programs in metropolitan areas
of the East and Midwest. "In each of the three residency
programs," they write, "we have felt that a preselection
process is operant that by design or otherwise limits the
number of black patients initially seen and those ultimately
treated. Part of this preselection process involves the referring
person or agency, which is aware that the clinic is interested
in 'good' treatment cases. 'Good' refers to young, motivated,
introspective patients with few reality difficulties who are students, suburban housewives, upwardly striving junior execu-
tives, or others with whom it is relatively easy to identify.
Thus the referring agency is likely to send white middle class
people who they feel can benefit from psychotherapy."

The referral agencies have learned their lesson well. For
the fact is that many psychiatric clinics do resist taking black
patients. These clinics assume that black persons are poor
candidates for intensive psychotherapy and support this notion by invoking psychoanalytic theory. "This theory stresses
that those people who will benefit from intensive psychotherapy are those whose ego strengths of motivation, intelligence,
introspection, delay of gratification, and repudiation of action
in favor of thinking are rated highly. Invariably a black person is rated as having few of the desired ego strengths and is
therefore not a good candidate for anything more than the
supportive therapies. We feel that too many intake workers

are not empathic enough to make accurate assessments of black patients because they are unable or unwilling to deal with the subtleties and nuances present in the material presented by these patients" (Jones *et al.*, 1970). Thus, in the institutions described by the five psychiatrists, very few of the black patients admitted were given individual or group psychotherapy, the most valued modalities of treatment in the institutions involved. Most black patients were assigned to forms of treatment considered second-best by the professional staff: drug clinics, 15-minute clinics, or medical student training programs with a rapid turnover of inexperienced therapists.

Institutional facilities for treatment of black patients are notoriously inadequate in ghetto areas. These areas are serviced mainly by municipal clinics and hospitals that are grossly underbudgeted and understaffed. As with schools and housing, most physical plants are antiquated. Such deficiencies affect disadvantaged white patients too, of course, but they hit with greatest force the black poor in the cities.

"The absence of the private or public psychiatrist from the predominantly black inner city long ago dropped him from the list of potentially available mental health resources for the urban slum school child or working class adult," observe Dr. Sabshin and his colleagues at the University of Illinois (Sabshin *et al.*, 1970). In their fine review of institutional racism in psychiatry, they emphasize that the glaring disparity in the number of physicians available in poverty and middle-class areas is especially marked in regard to psychiatrists and neurologists.

2

The decision as to who gets to the hospital may hinge on a person's color rather than the degree of his mental disturbance. Often it is the police department that determines whether an individual is to be hospitalized or jailed. In Baltimore, for instance, the police play a major role in routing patients—44% of adult Baltimoreans admitted to Maryland's state mental hospitals are taken there by the police department, and "Emergency psychiatric services at both the University of Maryland and Johns Hopkins evaluate only one third the number of patients committed by police surgeons from the city jail" (Schleifer *et al.*, 1968). One hardly expects that the training and viewpoint of the police would alert them to the possibility of psychiatric disorder in a black who comes to their attention. "The police, as an agency of social control, are more likely to view less disturbed behavior as a delinquent act rather than a manifestation of illness. Therefore patients with less florid symptomology are returned without treatment to trial and then to jail or the community. Our findings suggest that Negroes need to display greater behavioral disorganization or more dramatic sickness before the police relinquish control and turn the individual over to a hospital for treatment" (Schleifer *et al.*, 1968).

The black psychiatric patient is less likely than the white to be admitted to a hospital or to receive outpatient treatment in the early stages of mental illness (Bahn *et al.*, 1966). Moreover, even when referred to a clinic, he will on the average be treated for a shorter period of time than a white patient (Schleifer *et al.*, 1968). "It is difficult," reported one team of investigators, "to explain the greater services offered white than non-white patients in terms of medical requirements. This clearly suggests that social and other factors rather than diagnostic needs may be a major consideration" (Bahn *et al.*, 1962). That is putting it mildly.

The psychiatrist cannot wash his hands of this problem. He must do what he can, in terms of his own professional position, to foster equitable treatment. He has his own leverages: his position in the profession, in the administrative establishment, and in the community.

3

In his own work with patients, the psychiatrist has the obligation to rid himself of any bias that affects his judgment as to who should go into treatment or be hospitalized—and what kind of treatment should be administered. If he regards black persons as "naturally" impulsive or emotional, he may decide that certain modes of behavior are not of psychiatric concern when they in fact reflect mental illness. Or he may commit the opposite error. If the clinician fails to take into account special environmental circumstances, he will misjudge normal behavior as pathological. He may label realistic anger as neurotic hostility: or he may mechanically accept an IQ test report that rates the patient as "mentally retarded," not recognizing the cultural bias built into the test.

To avoid such errors, the psychiatrist must be acutely aware at all times of how profoundly the social environment can influence patterns of behavior. Unfortunately, however, such awareness has led some psychiatrists to adopt a nihilistic attitude toward the treatment of poor blacks. They contend that it is hopeless to treat a person who will continue to live in a pathogenic environment. Some even argue that the problems of a black patient are so bound up with his oppression by the white power structure that he cannot be truly helped until racism has been wiped out. No matter what the good will of persons who take this position, they are in effect shutting the door of treatment facilities on patients with emotional problems or mental illness. The attitude appears militant, but is actually a counsel of exclusion. The white psychiatrist would never think of adopting such a "revolutionary" do-nothing stand toward his white patients.

The fact is that not all the psychiatric problems that may trouble black persons derive from the racist arrangement. To think otherwise is to dehumanize the black person, to deny that like other persons he has conflicts, ambivalences, a capacity for being stimulated or dulled by the innumerable hazards of life. These problems would obviously not vanish with the establishment of a just society, any more than all medical problems would disappear. It is of course true that both psychiatric and physiologic problems are exacerbated and sometimes even produced by poverty and discrimination. But it is idly utopian to deny that some difficulties are part of the human condition. Many mental aberrations have a bio-chemical basis. Others may be due to genetic abnormalities. Still others stem from dissonant interpersonal relations that cannot always be so artfully arranged that they are guaranteed to avoid distress. In any case, even if all psychiatric difficulties were due to racism, it would be irrational and inhumane to withhold whatever strategies of intervention are currently available.

One may therefore be wary of those who advise the psychiatrist that a concern with the mental problems of the black patient is a diversion from the fight against the racist society that generates such problems. The psychiatrist has a dual responsibility. He must participate in the larger fight against racism, together with other citizens. He also has a specific professional responsibility to the black patient. His good will is worth little if it is applied in every area but that of his special competence. The patient will hardly appreciate his doctor's community activities if these are used to justify neglect of his own individual problems.

Psychotherapy for a marital or a work problem may have a positive effect even though it cannot eliminate the adverse social setting within which the stress developed. By helping the individual mobilize his potentially healthy psychological forces, the various therapeutic modalities may make a real difference in his functioning. To deny treatment on the ground that it is merely putting a patch on an environmental abscess is to acquiesce in current discriminatory practices, even if with radical-sounding rhetoric. Rather, the call for social action should be combined with the demand for an adequate number of properly staffed and financed treatment facilities.

To advocate such facilities is not by itself a sufficient response to the problem. Perhaps even more crucial is the issue of how these facilities are to be used. What will be their function and purpose? The bias against psychiatry expressed by many militants is altogether understandable in light of the conventional emphasis on "adjustment" as the goal of therapy. Frantz Fanon, who was both a revolutionary and a psychiatrist, rightly observed that a psychiatry that sought to induce adjustment to oppression would itself be pathologic. The function of therapy is hopelessly distorted by those who would persuade the patient to "live with" (that is, accept and yield to) indefensible social imperatives.

It is true that conflicts between an individual's life style and the dominant patterns of society create psychological stress. Psychiatrists who advocate adjustment assume that such stress is unhealthy and should be eliminated. Since social norms cannot be changed overnight, the individual must learn to conform to the prevailing scheme of things. Stated thus bluntly, this thesis would be disowned by most psychiatrists. Nevertheless, the model of adjustment is pervasive in actual clinical practice, as the psychiatric literature abundantly testifies. The concept that deviation from the conventional norm is pathological becomes manifest in the readiness to label student activists and black militants as emotionally disturbed. In view of this, one can understand a certain distrust of psychiatry as an instrument in the service of the Establishment.

But a different approach to "adjustment" is possible in psychiatry. Stress and conflict are part of normal life, and the process of growth implies a clash between habitual ways of behaving and the need for new modes of functioning. The consequences of stress are not necessarily destructive. Struggle against racism is stressful, no doubt, but it is also healthy. The attempt to eliminate stress (to "adjust") by yielding to racism and accepting a role of inferiority is unhealthy. The purpose of therapy is not adjustment but more effective functioning. And one aspect of such functioning is involvement in the struggle against social injustices that violate the integrity of one's existence.

4

In the biracial patient-therapist relationship, a number of special problems arise. Our own experience makes it necessary to limit the present discussion to the situation in which a white therapist treats a black patient.*

The white psychiatrist may easily fall into major errors in his approach. One is the illusion of color blindness, the assumption that the black person is "just another patient." This has a fine impartial ring, but it is also hollow. For like all proclamations of "color-blindness" it seeks to abstract the black man from the specific conditions of his history and existence in the United States. The primary consequence of this fallacy is to automatically label deviations from the white middle-class standard as evidence of intrapsychic pathology.

The opposite error is the assumption that all of the patient's problems revolve around the condition of being black. As one example, consider the case of a black man who came to one of the authors (A.T.) because of psychoneurotic disturbances after a previous period of unsuccessful treatment elsewhere. The other therapist had approached the patient with the attitude that a lifetime of oppression had produced a permanent crippling of his personality. In effect, the patient had been told that this was a great injustice, it was not his fault, but nevertheless it was true. Though expressed subtly, this derogation of the patient's basic personality had been unmistakably communicated to him. This led to progressive alienation of the patient, culminating in the rupture of the therapeutic relationship. In the new treatment situation the patient was evaluated as having impressive evidences of a normal, healthy aspect to his personality structure, as indicated by the way he functioned in his work and personal life. His psychoneurotic difficulties had arisen out of the particular family constellation in which he grew up, as it might with any other

---

* For reports of the clinical experiences of black psychiatrists with both black and white patients, see among others, Grier (1967), Grier and Cobbs (1968), Schachter and Butts (1968), Calnek (1970).

person. The discrimination he suffered as a black man had served to intensify his neurotic patterns but had in no way "deformed" him psychologically. This approach made a profound difference in the therapeutic outcome.

With great foresight, Viola Bernard (1953) cautioned her fellow psychoanalysts nearly 20 years ago against the danger that they would perpetuate "a new form of racial stereotype —the psychoanalytic stereotype—i.e., the Negro personality whose frustrated hostility towards whites must always automatically constitute his central conflict and the core of his personality organization." Dr. Bernard pointed out that "Negroes, struggling against the standard racial stereotypes, are understandably alarmed by the threat of such a sophisticated new version of racial stereotypy, under the aegis of psychodynamics." Unfortunately, this thoughtful warning was not widely heeded, and "the psychoanalytic stereotype" did indeed become part of the professional stock-in-trade.

Some clinicians tend to avoid discussions about race either because they are uncomfortable about the subject, unclear about their own views, or fearful that such discussions will be painful to the patient. This can happen in the treatment of children as well as of adults. In a perceptive discussion of this issue, Dr. Paul L. Adams, Professor of Psychiatry and Pediatrics at the University of Florida, writes: "The child psychiatry resident who is white, and humanely liberal in politics, may object to discussing blackness and whiteness with black children. It is as if blackness were a more distasteful topic than incestuous wishes, which the resident might be eager to consider. Wishing to 'spare the child with a confrontation about skin color' the resident will direct all his energies away from talk of color. However, the resident can be led to realize that a black child's world contains his blackness; and that an open consideration of this fact yields more than denial and anxious evasion" (Adams, 1970). To gloss over race in a racist society may in itself be a capitulation to racism.

Another distortion of the psychotherapeutic process may

occur in relation to the "transference" phenomenon. The term
transference is used by psychiatrists to designate the irrational
and inappropriate attitudes that a patient may develop toward
the therapist. Identification of this process can play an important role in treatment. The danger is that a white psychiatrist may ignore the possibility that the black patient's critical
reactions to him have a realistic foundation. The therapist cannot assume that his own training has given him an objectivity
that guarantees freedom from all racist ideology and feeling.
And it is arrogant for the psychiatrist to expect the black
patient to respond to him as if he were an Olympian figure
untouched by the world around him. If the patient is upset by
having his dreams or emotions characterized as "primitive,"
his objection may not be an irrational one arising out of neurosis but an appropriate reflection of his life experience with
racism. This reaction may properly be termed "pseudo-transference" (Thomas, 1962)—in other words, a realistic response
to a racist bias in the therapist which is misinterpreted as
neurotic.

5

The standard forms of treatment, however one may judge
their individual merits, should be available to black patients
on an equal basis with whites. But there is the further issue
of developing modes of therapy designed to meet the special
needs of the urban poor. The conventional modalities were
largely based on the needs of white middle-class patients. It
is necessary to build new models that are pertinent for the
inner-city population of the 1970's.

Traditional methods of delivering care to the neighborhood,
based on the mental hygiene clinic, the hospital, and the community social agency, have been unsatisfactory in several
major respects. For one thing, the responsibility for such care
has been fragmented. The division of authority and function
among state, city, and private agencies has resulted in an
uncoordinated patchwork of services. There has been con-

siderable overlapping between agencies as well as faulty inter-communication.

Another serious problem is lack of continuity and comprehensiveness of care. A patient who requires different kinds of treatment is shuttled from one service to another. Many clinics are open only during the day, so that an outpatient who needs immediate help outside of office hours may be left helpless in a threatening situation. The patient should have available in one neighborhood center all the modalities of service he may need, and he should be able to secure such services around the clock.

In addition, the community itself has had little or no say in determining the kind of services that may be most useful to its residents. The community must have an organized way of making its experiences and judgments felt.

While all of these issues are important for the general population, they most directly affect the poor and black communities. The affluent family can draw on private psychiatric resources to insure continuity and comprehensiveness of care.

Various patterns of delivering psychiatric care are being developed in different communities. These new models must meet many tests, but none is more critical than their effectiveness in overcoming racist preconceptions and practices.

11

Challenge to the Profession

I

THE ISSUE OF RACISM in the mental health profession was brought to a head in the late 1960's at annual meetings of the American Psychiatric Association, the American Psychological Association, the American Orthopsychiatric Association, and other leading organizations in this field. At these meetings, caucuses of black members demanded that the associations not only overhaul their own structures but also take an active part in the struggle to end discrimination throughout the profession.

The initiative and persistence of the black caucuses spurred a long overdue re-examination of basic attitudes and practices on the part of white mental health workers. As never before, these workers were forced to take a serious look at the extent to which racism had infected their own ranks. The black challenge shattered the illusions of many that their commitment to mental health and integration shielded them from racist influences that are so pervasive in American society.

In a representative action, some 100 black psychiatrists at the 1969 meeting of the American Psychiatric Association (marking the A.P.A.'s 125th anniversary) called on the organization to end the traditional "exclusion of blacks from positions of influence and authority." They asked the A.P.A. to insist that psychiatry departments recruit more black residents and faculty, and make professional training more relevant to the needs of black people. They demanded that the National

146

Institute of Mental Health "change its whole stance, vis-à-vis the black community"—in hiring practices, financing mechanisms, use of black consultants, and program development. The A.P.A. was also urged to ensure desegregation of all public and private mental health facilities, and to deny or revoke the membership of any psychiatrist who refuses to treat black patients, maintains a segregated office, or works in a segregated or discriminatory facility.

The justice of these demands was recognized by the A.P.A.'s Board of Trustees, which endorsed the "general spirit of reform and redress of racial inequities in American psychiatry" and pledged to act in this spirit. Implementation of this pledge would indeed have a liberating influence on theory and practice in American psychiatry.

The issues raised by the black psychiatrists are by no means limited to matters of internal organization, important as these are. The entire range of psychiatric activities is now under scrutiny, including patterns of professional training, research, referrals, and delivery of mental health services. As the black professionals detail their own experiences in published papers, the specific ways in which racism manifests itself, whether grossly or subtly, become ever more clear.

2

To begin with, there is the pressing need to recruit and train black psychiatrists. Medical education in general has been a "tightly segregated system," notes Dr. James L. Curtis, Associate Dean at the Cornell University Medical School, in his *Blacks, Medical Schools, and Society* (Curtis, 1971). Up to a few years ago, the two predominantly black medical schools (Howard University College of Medicine and Meharry Medical College) graduated nearly 85% of the black doctors, while 99 predominantly white schools, with superior resources of funds and facilities, graduated a token number. This dual system of medical education in America is being significantly modified, and in 1970 about half of all black medical students attended predominantly white schools. A number of leading medical schools are even competing for gifted black students. In 1968, there were 266 black medical students enrolled; in 1970 the number had risen to 697.

These gains are welcome, but we have a long way to go. Though black Americans make up 11.03% of the population, in 1969 they made up 2.75% of the 38,000 medical students and only 2.2% of the 230,000 practicing physicians (Curtis, 1971).

In psychiatry, too, there have been gains that mark only a beginning. Dr. Curtis recalls that when he graduated from medical school 25 years ago, he hesitated a long time as a black man before specializing in psychiatry. Opportunities for residencies in this field, as indeed in other specialties, were few and far between for blacks—"There were in fact only eight Negro psychiatrists in the whole country." Even today, blacks make up about 1% of all psychiatrists, and a 1971 survey suggested that they represented only 2% of the psychiatric residents.

The need to expand career opportunities for black psychiatrists is not simply a matter of elementary justice to young people now denied a chance to fulfill their talent. It is also vital for improving public mental health in America. The untapped reservoir of black youth is especially important in developing and administering programs in the black community.

The argument is often heard that not enough young blacks are really qualified to pursue a medical career, and that they would be more than welcome if only they were equipped. This is usually a rationalization for carrying on business as usual. The argument evades the responsibility of medical educators to help black students who may need extra encouragement and training to overcome handicaps imposed by racist pressures. As Dr. Chester M. Pierce, professor of education and psychiatry at Harvard, suggests: "To get more Negroes to go to medical school, we must find a way to let the Negro child know that it is possible for him to become a doctor, that he will be received by both the community and his peers, that he has the ability to get through school and that there are easy ways for him to finance his education. Perhaps the most important need we have is to find a truly creative way of letting children know that there are exciting, worthwhile gratifications in being a psychiatrist. Getting more Negroes to medical school may require curriculum changes as well as intensive recruiting. . . . As we attempt to do things to increase the level of training in secondary schools we must begin to think about special programs and newer teaching methods in order to get the more disadvantaged youth into medical specialties. Our overall task is to think out such programs and articulate our expectation that they will be financed and instituted" (Pierce, 1968).*

Similar problems exist in related fields. A survey by the American Psychological Association's Committee on Equality of Opportunity in Psychology indicates that between 1920 and 1966 blacks received less than 1% of the doctorates in psychology granted by the 25 universities giving the largest number of such degrees. If there were any Ivy League Ph.D.s in psychology, they were not represented among the black psychologists responding to the Committee's questionnaire. The median annual salary of these respondents was 32% less than that of white psychologists in 1966. Many described their isolation from the mainstream of the profession. The "inescapable conclusion" was that "being a Negro psychologist may reduce the handicap of being black, but it does not remove it" (Wispé et al., 1969). Another study concluded that "While it is true that many graduate departments of psychology in predominantly white colleges are trying to recruit black students, it is not clear as to how much effort they are putting into recruiting black undergraduates to become psychology majors" (Bayton

* Cutbacks in federal support for medical students and psychiatric residents have tragic consequences for the mental health field in general. For blacks and other minorities the effects of such cuts are nothing short of disastrous.

. The problem is aggravated by the limited re-
 predominantly black colleges. A survey of 14
 ...tions in this category reveals that only four have
...er's degree programs in psychology, and only one of
these has a Ph.D. program.

3

The problem does not end with admission of blacks to
graduate studies, specifically medical schools and psychiatric
residency programs, as we are reminded in the report, already
cited, by five black psychiatrists (Jones *et al.*, 1970) who describe their experiences as residents in three predominantly
white training institutes. Blacks chosen to enter such programs
are expected to share the institution's white middle-class values
and "demonstrate that they will uphold, continue to support,
and reaffirm the white institution's concept of itself as liberal,
unbiased, and nondiscriminatory." Those who appear to challenge these views are considered unsuitable candidates. If accepted for training, the black resident is subject to an almost
"hallucinatory whitening" by officials who insist that "color
doesn't matter." Patronizing attitudes are rife—"The black resident receives high praise for what would be considered ordinary
achievement by other residents, and there is a reluctance to
criticize him for his shortcomings." If the black resident reacts
against displays of racism he is labeled as hypersensitive about
race. "We may even say that when questions of racism come
up the black resident is expected to deal with them as if he
were himself white, lest he disturb the apparent peaceful black-
white relations."

Supervisors in the training institutes, the authors report,
are mainly white psychiatrists, many of whom have never
treated a black patient. Most supervisors minimize the influence of sociological factors on personality development. The
few who do deal forthrightly with the issue are able to make
a positive contribution. "The supervisor who confronts us immediately with what he notices first and our patient notices

first—our blackness—is the most helpful. This confrontation, which can immediately change the nature of the supervisory process, is an important influence on the treatment of the patient we are presenting to him, whether the patient is black or white."

Urging that black psychiatrists be sought out and utilized as participants in the training of residents, the authors observe that "Black supervisors would be as useful to the white residents in our programs as to us in helping all of us consider the special contribution of racism and discrimination to the psyche of both white and black patients." This problem is linked to the patient-selection process which tends to screen out blacks as unsuitable for intensive, long-term psychotherapy. "The major problem in this area is the loss to us, as well as to other residents and the institution, of a chance to understand the black patient and the unique problems he may present. Such policies also prevent us from observing and understanding the strength and methods of adaptation of a suppressed and oppressed minority."

4

Another professional area that requires a new approach is the referral procedure of white psychiatrists. Overcrowded schedules in private practice often make it necessary to refer new patients to other therapists. What is the attitude of white psychiatrists toward sending patients to black psychiatrists? The subject of referral practices is always a touchy one for private practitioners and it is hardly surprising that the professional literature has bypassed it. The issue has been posed by two black psychiatrists (Harrison and Butts, 1970), who sent a questionnaire on the subject to 100 white and black clinicians practicing in New York, Detroit, and Chicago. There were 42 responses, and the authors suggest that "The failure of many white psychiatrists to respond may have reflected their anxiety about the topic and their reluctance to deal with it."

In the survey, destructive racial attitudes among white therapists were revealed in a variety of ways, including the following:

1) Failure to refer to a black psychiatrist because of overconcern that he would be "humiliated" and "hurt" by the patient's attitudes, which the therapist would be unable to cope with.

2) Reluctance of white psychiatrists to recognize or to point out to patients that racial prejudice is an unhealthy symptom.

3) Feelings that black psychiatrists are better able to treat children, adolescents, and hippies than middle-class white adults.

The questionnaire also confirmed that fee considerations play an important part. Some white psychiatrists have developed a theory that their black colleagues are better able to treat working-class patients, especially blacks. Such modesty would be more becoming if it were not a rationalization for rejecting patients who cannot pay high fees.

The questionnaire sent out by Harrison and Butts also elicited comments by white psychiatrists who had been taught by black psychiatrists. A number reported that their initial reaction had been misgivings about the ability of the black professional to teach or evaluate them, and that they were "relieved" to discover that he was competent. They also acknowledged holding certain stereotypes about black psychiatrists, such as that they "are tied up in exploring and exploiting black/white situations," "are trying to work out past problems and change them a bit," or "are a little whiter than most blacks."

In view of this, it is significant that of the white psychiatrists polled, only one-half said that they had black friends. "This lack of social opportunity for modifying racial stereotypes," the authors observe, "contributes to the ineffectiveness of white psychiatrists, not only with black patients, but in the referral of white patients to black psychiatrists."

Harrison and Butts make two major recommendations. One is that white psychiatrists should confront patients honestly and directly with regard to their racial stereotypes and the psychological harm caused by prejudiced thinking. A patient's reluctance to be referred to a competent black therapist should be openly challenged. "Patients with questions or ambivalence about black psychiatrists need a definitive, reassuring statement by the white psychiatrist, not just an exploration of their feelings." Secondly, the white psychiatrist himself should strive to overcome his isolation from meaningful associations with black people. "A broadening of professional and social relationships increases the knowledge of others and self-knowledge."

5

Still another area in which the mental health professional must do some basic re-thinking is that of research. The need for this may not seem obvious to many workers. It has been assumed that research on any aspect of the effects of racism on blacks is commendable in itself and expresses a commitment to the struggle against racism. This assumption is now being vigorously challenged. The criticism goes beyond the usual issues of methodology, sampling, and interpretation. What is now under question is the subject matter and direction of the research.

The time has come to shift the focus of study, says Elizabeth Herzog (1971), one of the most astute investigators in this field. As she points out, the black community is rebelling against "proliferating questionnaires and swarming investigators." Blacks are sick and tired of playing the role of psycho-social guinea pig, especially since the energy that goes into research is not matched by action to change conditions. But the most important reason for shifting the focus is that in order to learn what we now need to know "we must look at different people and situations, and pose different questions."*

The present emphasis on studying the poor and the blacks implies that these are the "problem" groups. The real problem resides in the haves rather than the have-nots. What stands in the way of social advance is resistance to change on the part of the rich and powerful, their reluctance to give up even a tiny fraction of their privileges. "If we could really document among the 'haves' the full extent to which the money-prestige-status complex dominates our society, it might be as shocking as the documentation we have witnessed of racism, poverty, hunger, and pollution. This is one message that the dissident young are trying to shout into our ears" (Herzog, 1971).

In a probing editorial on "Research and the Black Backlash," Comer (1970) notes that many social scientists blame the black community for "irrational behavior" because it resents being treated as a target of research. Some professionals view this backlash as a ploy to gain control of funds expended in programs of research and intervention. Instead, these professionals should look at their own scientific blindspots, says Comer. "Have social scientists and their institutions been as ethical and responsible with the data they have collected as they should have been?" Comer asks, citing Arthur Jensen's sweeping speculations about the genetic inferiority of black intelligence. Comer also challenges those social scientists who don't even know what questions to ask and what variables to test since their ignorance of black life is just about total. One consequence of this ignorance is a focus on pathology, with little or no research on the positive adaptations and strengths of blacks. The stress has been on individual failings rather than on system deficiencies. And Comer also asks the important question: How are professional organizations using re-

---

* As the late Whitney Young once observed, "In fact, the Negro-studying business has become so big that I'm afraid if we just end it quickly, too many people will be thrown out of work. I'd like to propose a study of white folks. After all, Negroes didn't create the ghetto, white folks did" (*National Observer*, April 1, 1968).

search findings to influence social policy in a way to benefit the community?

Careful and responsible scholarship must be cherished, as Comer points out, but "much research, interpretation, and reporting in the area of black and white differences probably falls short of being careful and responsible—even falls short of being good research." One problem is that research careers have been virtually closed to black professionals. This point has also been emphasized by Pierce (1970): "The public and private patrons of research now must be persuaded that it is crucial, even in times of a threatened cutback of research funds, to make special plans to encourage and develop black researchers."

6

Even more urgent than the reordering of research is the mental health professional's commitment to the upgrading of patient services in the black community. There is a pressing need for new approaches that are relevant to the crisis of the inner city. A start—it is only that—has been made with the setting up of community mental health centers. Even the limited experience with such centers, and specifically those in or near black neighborhoods, has made it clear that actual involvement in the life of the community is essential to the success of the psychiatrist's efforts. He can function effectively only in collaboration with community organizations. And he cannot benefit from such collaboration if he comes into the community simply to tell people what is good for them. He must learn to listen.

This may not be easy for psychiatrists accustomed to listening from a superior position. As Viola W. Bernard (1971), a prominent psychoanalyst, observes, "Some of the most taxing interracial experiences for some white psychiatrists have been occurring in community mental health programs in which they have been involved in urban ghetto areas. There, they have been subjected to anti-white rage and contemptuous repudiation by groups of black residents—a situation for which their prior sense of professional identity and experience had in no way prepared them." The question, says Dr. Bernard, is: "Will such situations intensify the already existing white racism within psychiatry or will they lead to its reduction?" There is a real danger of "backlash" on the part of some white mental health workers who are not really prepared to challenge their own preconceptions and prejudices. But Dr. Bernard is hopeful that "those who are able to recognize and accept that there is some reality core in this open hostility to whites as such, can make use of that knowledge to help uproot the legacy of racism that plagues us."

One positive response to the problem is that reported by Bernard Bandler (1969), who headed a university effort to develop a community health center in Roxbury, Mass. On the basis of his experience there, Dr. Bandler views community confrontation as "the extraordinary process by which the black community intentionally educates the white community. . . . It parallels analysis in the intensity of feelings aroused, the need to understand oneself . . . and for the non-black, it is the ideal educational method for beginning to understand black people and the black community."

Another positive example is offered by Dr. Irving N. Berlin, co-director of social and community psychiatry at the University of Washington in Seattle. Reporting on a troubled situation that aroused strong feelings in a ghetto area, he points out that active participation of health workers, not operating as outsiders looking in, proved salutary to them as well as the community. Unfortunately, the present training of most health workers does not put them in a position to place their skills at the service of the community and its objectives. "It is clear," Dr. Berlin (1971) says, "that their psychodynamic understanding of individuals, while helpful in individual work, cannot be applied to the community in undigested form. Some of the omnipotence characteristic of mental health professionals is clearly designed to turn off any community organization with which they might be involved."

The challenge to the psychiatric profession has been effectively summed up in a report by a group of University of Illinois professors (Sabshin, Diesenhaus, and Wilkerson, 1970): "Current psychiatric structures do not seem viable for rapidly producing the changes necessary to eradicate institutional racism. New 'counterstructures' are required in which black professionals and consumers truly share with whites in the determination of all service practices. Institutional racism is a subtle phenomenon; white psychiatrists functioning as they have in the past can continue to act to reinforce the myth of black inferiority while espousing equality. It is the commitment to change and the implementing of behavior that flows from this commitment that will determine whether American psychiatry will continue to manifest institutional racism. . . .

"We are asking white psychiatrists to become increasingly aware of how their everyday practices continue to perpetuate institutional white racism in psychiatry and to support the search for realistic solutions to providing psychiatric services to black people. We ask white psychiatrists to provide strong sanction and support to these efforts. This means making available the necessary resources of money, manpower, and authority—and not just in the current token accounts. It means not defending the vested white interests in old institutional forms of professionalism when new strategies and roles are suggested; it means relinquishing negative stereotypes of the black patient; it means truly sharing administrative decision-making with black colleagues and black communities."

Only such a total commitment, only such a determined redirection of thought and effort, can fulfill the white psychiatrist's obligation as a scientist and a citizen to combat the inhuman destructiveness of racism in our society.

References

ABRAHAMSEN, D., 1970. *Our Violent Society*. New York: Funk and Wagnalls.

ACKERMAN, N. W., 1970. What happened to the family? *Mental Hygiene*, 54:459-463.

ADAMS, P. L., 1970. Dealing with racism in biracial psychiatry. *Journal of the American Academy of Child Psychiatry*, 9:33-43.

ADORNO, T. W., E. FRENKEL-BRUNSWIK, D. J. LEVINSON, and R. N. SANFORD, 1950. *The Authoritarian Personality*. New York: Harper.

ALEXANDER, F. G. and S. SELESNICK, 1966. *The History of Psychiatry*. New York: Harper & Row.

ALLPORT, G. W., 1954. *The Nature of Prejudice*. Reading, Mass.: Addison-Wesley.

————, 1961. *Pattern and Growth in Personality*. New York: Holt, Rinehart and Winston.

ANASTASI, A., 1958. *Differential Psychology: Individual and Group Differences in Behavior*. New York: Macmillan.

————, 1968. *Psychological Testing*, 3rd Ed. New York: Macmillan.

ANDREWS, J. B., 1887. The distribution and care of the insane in the United States. *Transactions of the International Medical Congress, Ninth Session*.

BABCOCK, J. W., 1895. The colored insane. *Alienist and Neurologist*, 16:423-447.

BAHN, A. K., C. A. CHANDLER, and L. EISENBERG, 1962. Diagnostic characteristics related to services in psychiatric clinics for children. *Milbank Memorial Fund Quarterly*, 40:289-318.

BAHN, A. K., E. A. GARDNER, L. ALTOP, 1966. Admission and prevalence rates for psychiatric facilities in four register areas. *American Journal of Public Health*, 56:2033-2051.

BANDLER, B., 1969. The reciprocal roles of the university and the community in the development of community mental health centers. In *How the Universities Can Aid Community-Health*, Proceedings of a Scientific Conference, University of Rochester, 63-75.

BARATZ, S. S. and J. C. BARATZ, 1970. Early childhood intervention: the social science basis of institutional racism. *Harvard Educational Review*, 40:29-50.

159

BAYLEY, N., 1970. Development of mental abilities. In Mussen, P. H. (Ed.): *Carmichael's Manual of Child Psychology*, 3rd ed. New York: Wiley.

BAYTON, J. A., O. S. ROBERTS, and R. K. WILLIAMS, 1970. Minority groups and careers in psychology. *American Psychologist*, 25: 504-510.

BEAN, R. B., 1906. Some racial peculiarities of the Negro brain. *American Journal of Anatomy*, 5:353-415.

BEISER, H. R., 1964. Discrepancies in the symptomatology of parents and children. *Journal of the Academy of Child Psychiatry*, 3:457-468.

BENEDICT, R., 1943. *Race: Science and Politics*. New York: Viking.

BENEDICT, R. and G. WELTFISH, 1943. *The Races of Mankind*. New York: Public Affairs Committee.

BERKELEY-HILL, O. A. R., 1924. The color question from a psychoanalytical viewpoint. *Psychoanalytical Review*, 11:246-253.

BERLIN, I. N., 1971. Professionals' participation in community activities: is it part of the job? *American Journal of Orthopsychiatry*, 41:494-500.

BERNARD, J., 1966. *Marriage and Family Among Negroes*. Englewood Cliffs, N. J.: Prentice Hall.

BERNARD, L. L., 1924. *Instinct: A Study in Social Psychology*. New York: Holt.

BERNARD, V. W., 1953. Psychoanalysis and members of minority groups. *Journal of the American Psychoanalytic Association*, 1:256-267.

————, 1971. Interracial practice in the midst of change. Paper read at the annual meeting of the American Psychiatric Association, Washington, D.C.

BERNSTEIN, B., 1960. Language and social class. *British Journal of Sociology*, 2:271-276.

BEVIS, W. M., 1921. Psychological traits of the Southern Negro with observations as to some of his psychoses. *American Journal of Psychiatry*, 1:69-78.

BILLINGSLEY, A., 1968. *Black Families in White America*. Englewood Cliffs, N. J.: Prentice-Hall.

————, 1970. Black families and white social science. *Journal of Social Issues*, 26:127-142.

BIRCH, H. G. and J. D. GUSSOW, 1970. *Disadvantaged Children: Health, Nutrition, and School Failure*. New York: Harcourt, Brace and World.

BIRD, B., 1957. A consideration of the etiology of prejudice. *Journal of the American Psychoanalytic Association*, 5:490-513.

BLAUNER, R., 1970. Black culture: myth or reality? In Whitten, N. E. and J. F. Szwed (Eds.), *Afro-American Anthropology: Contemporary Perspectives*. New York: The Free Press.

BLEULER, E. 1924. *Textbook of Psychiatry*. New York: Macmillan.

BLOOM, B. S., 1964. *Stability and Change in Human Characteristics*. New York: Wiley.

BRANHAM, E., 1970. One-parent adoptions. *Children*, 17:103-107.

BRIGHAM, C. C., 1923. *A Study of American Intelligence*. Princeton: Princeton University Press.

————, 1930. Intelligence tests of immigrant groups. *Psychological Review*, 37:158-165.

BRODY, E. B., 1966. Psychiatry and prejudice. In Arieti, S. (Ed.), *American Handbook of Psychiatry*, Volume 3. New York: Basic Books.

————, 1961. Social conflict and schizophrenic behavior in young adult Negro males. *Psychiatry*, 24:337-346.

————, 1963. Color and identity conflict in young boys: observations of Negro mothers and sons in urban Baltimore. *Psychiatry*, 26:188-201.

BROWN, L. L., 1951. Psychoanalysis vs. the Negro People. *Masses & Mainstream*, 4:16-24.

BROWN, S., 1969. A century of Negro portraiture. In Chametsky, J. and S. Kaplan (Eds.), *Black and White in American Culture*. Amherst: University of Massachusetts Press.

BUTTS, H. F., 1969. Review of Black Rage. *Journal of Negro Education*, 38:166-168.

CALNEK, M., 1970. Racial factors in the countertransference: the black therapist and the black client. *American Journal of Orthopsychiatry*, 40:39-46.

CAZDEN, C., 1970. The situation: a neglected source of social class differences in language use. *Journal of Social Issues*, 26:35-60.

CHESS, S., 1964. Mal de mère. *American Journal of Orthopsychiatry*, 34:613-614.

CHESS, S., K. B. CLARK, and A. THOMAS, 1953. The importance of cultural evaluation in psychiatric diagnosis and treatment. *Psychiatric Quarterly*, 27:102-114.

CLARK, K. B., 1955. *Prejudice and Your Child*. Boston: Beacon.

————, 1962. Educational stimulation of racially disadvantaged children. In Passow, A. H. (Ed.), *Education in Depressed Areas*. New York: Teachers College, Columbia University.

————, 1965. *Dark Ghetto*. New York: Harper & Row.

CLARK, K. B. and M. P. CLARK, 1939. The development of consciousness of self and emergence of racial identification in Negro preschool children. *Journal of Social Psychology*, 10:591-599.

————, 1947. Racial identification and preference in Negro children. In Newcomb, T. M. and E. L. Hartley (Eds.), *Readings in Social Psychology*. New York: Holt.

COLES, R., 1967. *Children of Crisis*. Boston: Little, Brown.

COLLINS, C. W., 1952. Psychoanalysis of groups: critique of a study of a small Negro sample. *Journal of the National Medical Association*, 44:165-171.

COMER, J. P., 1969. White racism: its root, form, and function. *American Journal of Psychiatry*, 126:802-806.

————, 1970. Research and the black backlash. *American Journal of Orthopsychiatry*, 40:8-11.

CRONBACH, L. J., 1969. Heredity, environment, and educational policy. *Harvard Educational Review*, 39:338-347.

CROW, J., 1969. Genetic theories and influences: comments on the value of diversity. *Harvard Educational Review*, 39:301-309.

CURTIS, J. L., 1971. *Blacks, Medical Schools, and Society*. Ann Arbor: The University of Michigan Press.

162   RACISM AND PSYCHIATRY

DAIN, N., 1964. *Concepts of Insanity in the United States, 1789-1865.* New Brunswick: Rutgers University Press.

DANIELS, R. and H. KITANO, 1970. *American Racism: Exploration of the Nature of Prejudice.* Englewood Cliffs, N. J.: Prentice-Hall.

DAVENPORT, C. B. and M. STEGGERDE, 1929. *Race Crossing in Jamaica,* Washington, D. C.

DAVIDSON, H. H. and J. W. GREENBERG, 1967. *School Achievers from a Deprived Background.* New York: The City College of the City University of New York.

DEUTSCH, A., 1944. The first U.S. census of the insane (1840) and its use as pro-slavery propaganda. *Bulletin of the History of Medicine,* 15:469-482.

DEUTSCH, M., 1969. Happenings on the way back to the forum: social science, IQ, and race differences revisited. *Harvard Educational Review,* 39:523-557.

DOBZHANSKY, T. 1962. *Mankind Evolving: The Evolution of the Human Species.* New Haven: Yale University Press.

DOLLARD, J., 1937. *Caste and Class in a Southern Town.* New Haven: Yale University Press.

DOLLARD, J., L. W. DOOB, N. E. MILLER, O. H. MOWRER, R. R. SEARS, C. S. FORD, C. I. HOVLAND, and R. T. SOLLENBERGER, 1939. *Frustration and Aggression.* New Haven: Yale University Press.

DOVENMUEHLE, R. H. and W. E. McGOUGH, 1965. Aging, culture and affect: predisposing factors. *International Journal of Social Psychiatry,* 11:138-146.

DU BOIS, W. E. B., 1897. Strivings of the Negro race. *Atlantic Monthly,* 80:197.

——— (Ed.), 1906. *The Health and Physique of the North American Negro.* Atlanta: The Atlanta University Press.

DUNN, L. C. and T. DOBZHANSKY, 1952. *Heredity, Race and Society.* Revised edition. New York: New American Library.

EHRLICH, P. H. and R. W. HOLM, 1964. A biological view of race. In A. Montagu (Ed.), *The Concept of Race.* New York: The Free Press.

ELLISON, R., 1967. A very stern discipline. *Harper's Magazine,* March, 76-95.

ENTWISLE, D. R., 1968. Developmental linguistics: inner-city children. *American Journal of Sociology,* 74:37-49.

EVARTS, A. B., 1914. Dementia praecox in the colored race. *The Psychoanalytical Review,* 1:388-403.

EYSENCK, H. J., 1971. *Race, Intelligence and Education.* London: Temple Smith.

FANON, F., 1967, *Toward the African Revolution.* New York: Grove Press.

FARIS, R. and H. W. DUNHAM, 1939. *Mental Disorders in Urban Areas.* Chicago: University of Chicago Press.

FARLEY, R. and A. I. HERMALIN, 1971. Family stability: a comparison of trends between blacks and whites. *American Sociological Review,* 36:1-17.

FISCHER, J., 1969. Negroes, whites and rates of mental illness: reconsideration of a myth. *Psychiatry,* 32:428-446.

FREEDMAN, A. M. and H. I. KAPLAN (Eds.), 1967. *Comprehensive Textbook of Psychiatry.* Baltimore: Williams & Wilkins.

FREUD, S., 1938. *The Basic Writings of Sigmund Freud.* Trans. by A. A. Brill. New York: Modern Library.
————, 1953. *A General Introduction to Psychoanalysis.* New York: Permabooks.
FRIED, M. H., 1968. The need to end the pseudoscientific investigation of race. In Mead, M. *et al.* (Eds.), *Science and the Concept of Race.* New York: Columbia University Press.
FRUMKIN, R. M., 1954. Race and mental disorders: a research note. *Journal of Negro Education,* 23:97-98.
FULLER, J. L. and W. R. THOMPSON, 1960. *Behavior Genetics.* New York: Wiley.
GARRETT, H. E., 1961. The equalitarian dogma. *Mankind Quarterly,* 1:253-257.
GEARHART, L. P. and D. B. SCHUSTER, 1971. Black is beautiful. *Archives of General Psychiatry,* 24:479-484.
GINSBERG, M., 1964. *The Psychology of Society.* London: Methuen.
GLAZER, N. and D. P. MOYNIHAN, 1963. *Beyond the Melting Pot.* Cambridge: M. I. T. Press.
GOLDSTEIN, N. F., 1948. *The Roots of Prejudice Against the Negro in the United States.* Boston: Boston University Press.
GOODENOUGH, F. L., 1926. Racial differences in intelligence of school children. *Journal of Experimental Psychology,* 9:388-397.
GOODENOUGH, F. L. and D. B. HARRIS, 1950. Studies in the psychology of children's drawings, II, 1928-1949. *Psychological Bulletin,* 47: 369-433.
GORDON, E. W. and D. A. WILKERSON, 1966. *Compensatory Educacate. IRCD Bulletin,* 5:1.
GORDON, E. W. and D. A. WILKERSON, 1966. *Compensatory Education for the Disadvantaged.* New York: College Entrance Examination Board.
GORDON. J. E., 1968. Book review. *American Journal of Orthopsychiatry,* 39:851-855.
GOSSETT, T. F., 1963. *Race: The History of an Idea in America.* Dallas: Southern Methodist University Press.
GRIER, W. H., 1967. When the therapist is Negro: some effects on the treatment process. *American Journal of Psychiatry,* 123:1587-1591.
GRIER, W. H. and P. M. COBBS, 1968. *Black Rage.* New York: Basic Books.
GROSS, H .S., *et al.,* 1969. The effect of race and sex on the variation of diagnosis and disposition in a psychiatric emergency room. *Journal of Nervous and Mental Disease,* 148:638-642.
GROSSACK, M. M. (Ed.), 1963. *Mental Health and Segregation.* New York: Springer.
GUILFORD, J. P., 1967. *The Nature of Human Intelligence.* New York: McGraw-Hill.
GULLATTEE, A. C., 1969. The Negro psyche: fact, fiction and fantasy. *Journal of the National Medical Association,* 61:119-129.
HALL, G. S., 1904. *Adolescence.* New York: Appleton.
————, 1905. The Negro in Africa and America. *Pedagogical Seminary,* 12:350-368.

————, 1923. *Life and Confessions of a Psychologist.* New York: Appleton.

HALLER, J. S., 1970 (a). The physician versus the Negro: medical and anthropological concepts of race in the late nineteenth century. *Bulletin of the History of Medicine,* 44:154-167.

————, 1970 (b). Concepts of race inferiority in nineteenth-century anthropology. *Journal of the History of Medicine,* 25:40-51.

HAMBURG, D. A., 1967. Report of ad hoc committee on central fact-gathering data. New York: American Psychoanalytic Association.

HAMILTON, J. W., 1967. Some dynamics of anti-Negro prejudice. *Psychoanalytic Review,* 53:5-15.

HANNERZ, U., 1969. *Soulside: Inquiries Into Ghetto Culture and Community.* New York: Columbia University Press.

HARRIS, M., 1968 (a). Race. In *International Encyclopedia of the Social Sciences.* New York: Macmillan.

————, 1968 (b). *The Rise of Anthropological Theory.* New York: Crowell.

HARRISON, P. A. and H. F. BUTTS, 1970. White psychiatrists' racism in referral practices to black psychiatrists. *Journal of the National Medical Association,* 62:278-282.

HENDIN, H., 1969. *Black Suicide.* New York: Basic Books.

HENSON, J., 1962. *Father Henson's Story of His Own Life.* New York: Corinth Books.

HERNTON, C. C., 1965. *Sex and Racism in America.* New York: Doubleday.

————, 1971. *Coming Together: Black Power, White Hatred and Sexual Hang-Ups.* New York: Random House.

HERZOG, E., 1971. Who should be studied? *American Journal of Orthopsychiatry,* 41:4-12.

HERZOG, E. and H. LEWIS, 1970. Children in poor families: myths and realities. *American Journal of Orthopsychiatry,* 40:375-387.

HERZOG, E. and C. E. SUDIA, 1968. Fatherless homes: a review of research. *Children,* Sept.-Oct., 177-182.

HESS, R. D., 1970. Social class and ethnic influences on socialization. In Mussen, P. H. (Ed.), *Carmichael's Manual of Child Psychology,* 3d ed., 2 vols. New York: Wiley.

HESS, R. D., V. C. SHIPMAN, J. BROPHY, and R. BEAR, 1968. *Cognitive Environments in Urban Preschool Children.* Chicago: The Graduate School of Education, University of Chicago.

HIGHAM, J., 1955. *Strangers in the Land: Patterns of American Nativism 1860-1925.* New Brunswick: Rutgers University Press.

HIRSCH, J., 1967. *Genetic Analysis.* New York: McGraw-Hill.

————, 1967. Behavior-genetic, or "experimental" analysis: the challenge of science versus the lure of technology. *American Psychologist,* 22:118-130.

————, 1970. Behavior genetic analysis and its biosocial consequences. *Seminars in Psychiatry,* 2:89-105.

HOCKING, F., 1970. Extreme environmental stress and its significance for psychopathology. *American Journal of Psychotherapy,* 24:4-26.

HOLLINGSHEAD, A. B. and F. C. REDLICH, 1958. *Social Class and Mental Illness.* New York: Wiley.

HOUSTON, S. H., 1970. A reexamination of some assumptions about the language of the disadvantaged child. *Child Development*, 41: 947-963.

HUNT, J. McV., 1971. Parent and child centers: their basis in the behavioral and educational sciences. *American Journal of Orthopsychiatry*, 41:13-38.

HUNTER, D. M. and C. G. BABCOCK, 1967. Some aspects of the intrapsychic structure of certain American Negroes as viewed in the intercultural dynamic. In Muensterberg, W. and S. Axelrad (Eds.), *The Psychoanalytic Study of Society*, Vol. 4. New York: International Universities Press.

JACO, E. G., 1960. *The Social Epidemiology of Mental Disorders*. New York: Russell Sage Foundation.

JARVIS, E., 1844. Insanity among the colored population of the free states. *American Journal of the Medical Sciences*, 7:71-83.

————, 1852. Insanity among the colored population of the free states. *American Journal of Insanity*, 8:268-282.

JASPERS, K., 1963. *General Psychopathology*. Chicago: Chicago University Press.

JENSEN, A. R., 1969. How much can we boost IQ and scholastic achievement? *Harvard Educational Review*, 39:1-123.

JOINT COMMISSION ON MENTAL HEALTH OF CHILDREN, 1970. *Crisis in Child Mental Health: Challenge for the 1970's*. New York: Harper & Row.

JONES, B. E., O. B. LIGHTFOOT, D. PALMER, R. G. WILKERSON, and D. H. WILLIAMS, 1970. Problems of black psychiatric residents in white training institutes. *American Journal of Psychiatry*, 127: 798-803.

JORDAN, W. D., 1968. *Black Over White: American Attitudes Toward the Negro, 1550-1812*. Chapel Hill: University of North Carolina Press.

JUNG, C. G., 1928. *Contributions to Analytical Psychology*. New York: Harcourt, Brace.

————, 1930. Your Negroid and Indian behavior. *Forum*, 83: 193-199.

KAGAN, J. S., 1969. Inadequate evidence and illogical conclusions. *Harvard Educational Review*, 39:274-277.

KAPLAN, S., 1949. The miscegenation issue in the election of 1864. *Journal of Negro History*, 36:284-285.

KARDINER, A. and L. OVESEY, 1951. *The Mark of Oppression*. New York: Norton. Paperback edition, 1962. New York: Meridian (World).

KARNO, M., 1966. The enigma of ethnicity in a psychiatric clinic. *Archives of General Psychiatry*, 14:516-520.

KATZ, I and P. GURIN (Eds.), 1969. *Social Science and Race Relations*, New York: Basic Books.

KLEE, G., *et al.*, An ecological analysis of diagnosed mental illness in Baltimore. In Monroe, R. R. *et al.* (Eds.), *Pychiatric Epidemiology and Mental Health Planning*. Washington, D. C.: American Psychiatric Association.

KENNEDY, J., 1952. Problems posed in the analysis of black patients. *Psychiatry*, 15:313-327. (Reprinted in Grossack, 1963.)

KLEINER, R. and S. PARKER, 1969. Social-psychological aspects of migration and mental disorder in a Negro population. *American Behavioral Scientist*, 13:104-125.

KLINEBERG, O., 1935. *Race Differences.* New York: Harper.

—————, 1944. *Characteristics of the American Negro.* New York: Harper.

—————, 1954. *Social Psychology.* New York: Holt.

—————, 1971. Black and white in international perspective. *American Psychologist*, 26:119-128.

KNOWLES, L. L. and K. PREWITT (Eds.), 1969. *Institutional Racism in America.* Englewood Cliffs, N. J.: Prentice-Hall.

KOLB, L. C., 1968. *Noyes' Modern Clinical Psychiatry*, 7th ed. Philadelphia: W. B. Saunders.

KOVEL, J., 1970. *White Racism: A Psychohistory.* New York: Pantheon.

LABOV, W., 1969. The logic of nonstandard dialect. In Alatis, J. (Ed.), *School of Languages and Linguistics Monograph Series*, No. 22, Georgetown University, 1-43.

LADNER, J. A., 1971. *Tomorrow's Tomorrow: The Black Woman.* New York: Doubleday.

LE BON, G. *The Psychology of Peoples.* London, 1898.

LEWIS, H., 1967. Culture, class, and family life among low-income urban Negroes. In Ross, A. M. and H. Hill (Eds.), *Employment, Race, and Poverty.* New York: Harcourt, Brace and World.

LEWIS, O., 1966. The culture of poverty. *Scientific American*, 215: 19-25.

LIDZ, T., 1968. *The Person.* New York: Basic Books.

LINCOLN, C. E., 1964. *My Face Is Black.* Boston: Beacon.

LIND, J. E., 1914. The dream as a simple wish-fulfillment in the Negro. *The Psychoanalytical Review*, 1:295-300.

LITWACK, L. F., 1961. *North of Slavery: The Negro in the Free States: 1790-1860.* Chicago: U. of Chicago Press.

LIVINGSTONE, F. R., 1962. On the nonexistence of races. *Current Anthropology*, 3:279-281.

MCCARTHY, J. D. and W. L. YANCEY, 1971. Uncle Tom and Mr. Charlie: metaphysical pathos in the study of racism and personal disorganization. *American Journal of Sociology*, 76:648-672.

MCCORD, W., J. HOWARD, B. FRIEDBERG, and E. HARWOOD, 1969. *Life Styles in the Black Ghetto.* New York: Norton.

MCDILL, E. L., E. D. MEYERS, JR., and L. RIGSBY, 1966. *Sources of Educational Climates in High Schools.* Baltimore: Department of Social Relations, Johns Hopkins University.

MCDOUGALL, W., 1908. *Social Psychology.* New York: Luce.

—————, 1921. *Is America Safe for Democracy?* New York: Scribner.

MCGURK, F., 1956. Psychological tests: a scientist's report on race differences. *U.S. News and World Report*, Sept. 21, 92-96.

MCLEAN, H. V., 1946. Psychodynamic factors in racial relations. *Annals of the Academy of Political and Social Science*, 244: 159-166.

MALL, F. P., 1909. On several anatomical characters of the human brain, said to vary according to race and sex. *American Journal of Anatomy*, 9:1-32.

MALZBERG, B., 1959. Mental disease among Negroes: an analysis of first admissions in New York State, 1949-1951. *Mental Hygiene*, 43:422-459.

MALZBERG, B. and E. S. LEE, 1956. *Migration and Mental Disease*. New York: Social Research Council.

MEAD, M., T. DOBZHANSKY, E. TOBACH, and R. E. LIGHT (Eds.), 1968. *Science and the Concept of Race*. New York: Columbia University Press.

METZGER, L. P., 1971. American sociology and black assimilation: conflicting perspectives. *American Journal of Sociology*, 76:627-647.

MONROE, R. R., G. D. KLEE, and E. B. BRODY (Eds.), *Psychiatric Epidemiology and Mental Health Planning*. Washington: American Psychiatric Association.

MONTAGU, A., 1964 (a). *Man's Most Dangerous Myth: The Fallacy of Race*, 4th revised ed. Cleveland: World.

———— (Ed.), 1964 (b). *The Concept of Race*. New York: The Free Press.

MORAIS, H. M., 1967. *The History of the Negro in Medicine*. New York: Publishers Co.

MYRDAL, G., 1944. *An American Dilemma: The Negro Problem and Democracy*, 2 vols. New York: Harper.

NEEL, J. V., 1970. Lessons from a "primitive" people. *Science*, 170: 815-822.

NEWBY, I. A., 1965. *Jim Crow's Defense: Anti-Negro Thought in America, 1900-1930*. Baton Rouge: Louisiana State University Press.

NOBLE, J. L., 1966. The American Negro Woman. In Davis, J. P. (Ed.), *The American Negro Reference Book*. Englewood Cliffs, N. J.: Prentice-Hall.

NOLEN, C. H., 1967. *The Negro's Image in the South: The Anatomy of White Supremacy*. Lexington: University of Kentucky Press.

NORTHUP, S., 1968. *Twelve Years a Slave*. Baton Rouge: University of Louisiana Press.

O'MALLEY, M., 1914. Psychoses in the colored race. *Journal of Insanity*, 71:309-336.

PARKER, S. and R. J. KLEINER, 1966. *Mental Illness in the Urban Ghetto Community*. Glencoe, Ill.: The Free Press.

PASAMANICK, B., 1963. Some misconceptions concerning differences in the racial prevalence of mental disease. *American Journal of Orthpsychiatry*, 33:72-86.

————, 1964. Myths regarding prevalence of mental disease in the American Negro. *Journal of the National Medical Association*, 56:6-17.

PASSOW, A. H. (Ed.), 1963. *Education in Depressed Areas*. New York: Teachers College, Columbia University.

PETTIGREW, T. F., 1964. *A Profile of the Negro American*. Princeton: Van Nostrand.

PIERCE, C. M., 1968. Manpower: the need for Negro psychiatrists. *Journal of the National Medical Association*, 60:30-33.

————, 1970. Research and careers for blacks. *American Journal of Psychiatry*, 127:817-818.

POSTELL, W. D., 1953. Mental health among the slave population in southern plantations. *American Journal of Psychiatry*, 110: 52-55.

POUSSAINT, A. F., 1968. The confessions of Nat Turner and the dilemma of William Styron. In Clarke, J. H. (Ed.), *William Styron's Nat Turner: Ten Black Writers Respond*. Boston: Beacon.

PRANGE, A. J. and M. M. VITOLS, 1962. Cultural aspects of the relatively low incidence of depression in southern Negroes. *International Journal of Social Psychiatry*, 8:104-112.

PROSHANSKY, H. and P. NEWTON, 1968. The nature and meaning of Negro self-identity. In Deutsch, M., I. Katz, and A. R. Jensen (Eds.), *Social Class, Race, and Psychological Development*. New York: Holt, Rinehart and Winston.

QUARLES, B., 1967. *Jet Magazine*, 33:32.

RAINWATER, L. and W. L. YANCEY, 1967. *The Moynihan Report and the Politics of Controversy*. Cambridge, Mass.: M.I.T. Press.

REDLICH, F. C. and FREEDMAN, D. X., 1966. *The Theory and Practice of Psychiatry*. New York: Basic Books.

RIESSMAN, F., 1962. *The Culturally Deprived Child*. New York: Harper.

ROBINSON, H. A., 1971. Pseudo-therapeutic benefits from an adverse social phenomenon (racial prejudice). *American Journal of Psychiatry*, 128:232-234.

RODMAN, H., 1968. Family and social pathology in the ghetto. *Science*, 161:756-762.

ROSENTHAL, R. and L. JACOBSON, 1968. *Pygmalion in the Classroom*. New York: Holt, Rinehart and Winston.

RUSH, B., 1799. Observations . . . *Transactions of the American Philosophical Society*, 4:289-297.

RYAN, W., 1965. Savage discovery: The Moynihan Report. *The Nation*, Nov. 22, 1965.

————, 1971. *Blaming the Victim*. New York: Pantheon.

SABSHIN, M., H. DIESENHAUS, and R. WILKERSON, 1970. Dimensions of institutional racism in psychiatry. *American Journal of Psychiatry*, 127:786-793.

SCHACHTER, J. S. and H. F. BUTTS, 1968. Transference and countertransference in interracial analyses. *Journal of the American Psychoanalytic Association*, 16:792-808.

SCHLEIFER, C. B., R. L. DERBYSHIRE, and J. MARTIN, 1968. Clinical change in jail-referred mental patients. *Archives of General Psychiatry*, 18:42-46.

SCHULTZ, C. B. and H. A. AUERBACH, 1971. The usefulness of cumulative deprivation of educational difficulties. *Merrill-Palmer Quarterly*, 17:27-39.

SCLARE, A., 1953. Cultural determinants in the neurotic Negro. *British Journal of Medical Psychology*, 26:278-288.

SHALER, N. S., 1890. The nature of the Negro. *Arena*, 3:23-25.

SHARPLEY, R. H., 1969. A psychohistorical perspective of the Negro. *American Journal of Psychiatry*, 126:645-650.

SHOCKLEY, W., 1966. Possible transfer of metallurgical and astronomical approaches to the problem of environment versus ethnic heredity. Quoted by Birch, H. G. in Mead *et al.*, *Science and the Concept of Race*, 1968.

SHUEY, A., 1958. *The Testing of Negro Intelligence*. Lynchburg, Va.: Bell.

SIEGEL, N. H., 1962. Characteristics of patients in psychoanalysis. *Journal of Nervous and Mental Disease*, 135:155-158.

SIGEL, I. E. and C. PERRY, 1968. Psycholinguistic diversity among culturally deprived children. *American Journal of Orthopsychiatry*, 38:122-126.

SIMON, R. I., 1965. Involutional psychosis in Negroes. *Archives of General Psychiatry*, 13:148-154.

SIMPSON, G. E. and J. M. YINGER, 1965. *Racial and Cultural Minorities: An Analysis of Prejudice and Discrimination*, 3rd ed. New York: Harper.

SLOBIN, D. I., 1968. Questions of language development in cross-cultural perspective. Paper prepared for symposium on "Language Learning in Cross-Cultural Perspective," Michigan State University.

SPUHLER, J. N. (Ed.), 1967. *Genetic Diversity and Human Behavior*. Chicago: Aldine.

SPUHLER, J. N. and G. LINDZEY, 1967. Behavioral differences between races. In Hirsch, J. (Ed.), *Behavior-Genetic Analysis*. New York: McGraw-Hill.

SPURLOCK, J., 1969. Problems of identification in young black children —static or changing. *Journal of the National Medical Association*, 61:504-507.

STAMPP, K. M., 1956. *The Peculiar Institution: Slavery in the Ante-Bellum South*. New York: Knopf.

STANTON, W., 1960. *The Leopard's Spots: Scientific Attitudes Toward Race in America, 1815-1859*. Chicago: University of Chicago Press.

STAPLES, R., 1970. The myth of the black matriarchy. *The Black Scholar*, Jan.-Feb.. 8-16.

———, 1971. The myth of the impotent black male. *The Black Scholar*, June, 2-9.

STERBA, R., 1947. Some psychological factors in Negro race hatred and in anti-Negro riots. In Roheim, G. (Ed.), *Psychoanalysis and the Social Sciences*, Vol. 1. New York: International Universities Press.

STEWART, W., 1969. Historical and structural bases for the recognition of Negro dialect. *School of Languages and Linguistics Monograph Series*, No. 22. Georgetown University, 239-247.

STOCKING, G. W., JR., 1968. *Race, Culture, and Evolution*. New York: The Free Press.

SULLIVAN, H. S., 1964. *The Fusion of Psychiatry and Social Science*. New York: Norton.

TENHOUTEN, W., 1970. The black family: myth and reality. *Psychiatry*, 33:145-173.

TERMAN, L. M., 1916. *The Measurement of Intelligence*. Boston: Houghton, Mifflin.

THOMAS, A., 1962. Pseudo-transference reactions due to cultural stereotyping. *American Journal of Orthopsychiatry*, 5:894-900.

THOMAS, A., M. E. HERTZIG, I. DRYMAN and P. FERNANDEZ, 1971. Examiner effect in IQ testing of Puerto Rican working-class children. *American Journal of Orthopsychiatry*, 41:809-821.

THOMAS, W. I., 1904. The psychology of race prejudice. *American Journal of Sociology*, 9:593-611.

TOBIAS, P. V., 1970. Brain-size, grey matter and race—fact or fiction? *American Journal of Physical Anthropology*, 32:3-26.

TONKS, C. M., E. S. PAYKEL, and G. L. KLERMAN, 1970. Clinical depression among Negroes. *American Journal of Psychiatry*, 127: 329-335.

VALENTINE, C. A., 1968. *Culture and Poverty: Critique and Counter-Proposals.* Chicago: University of Chicago Press.

VINCENT, C., 1966. Implications of changes in male-female role expectations for interpreting M-F scores. *Journal of Marriage and the Family*, 28:196-199.

WADDELL, K. J. and D. D. CAHOON, 1970. Comments on the use of the Illinois test of psycholinguistic abilities with culturally deprived children in the rural South. *Perceptual and Motor Skills*, 21: 56-58.

WASHBURN, S. L., 1963. The study of race. *American Anthropologist*, 65:521-523.

WEATHERLY, U. G., 1910. Race and marriage. *American Journal of Sociology*, 15:433-454.

WEINTRAUB, W. and H. ARONSON, 1968. A survey of patients in classical psychoanalysis. *Journal of Nervous and Mental Disease*, 146: 98-102.

WEXBERG, E., 1941. The comparative racial incidence (White and Negro) of neuropsychiatric conditions in a general hospital. *Tri-State Medical Journal*, 13:2694-2696.

WHITE, J., 1970. Guidelines for black psychologists. *The Black Scholar*, March, 52-57.

WHITE, W. A., 1903. Geographical distribution of insanity. *Journal of Nervous and Mental Disease*, 30:258-279.

WHITTEN, N. E. and J. F. SZWED (Eds.), 1970. *Afro-American Anthropology: Contemporary Perspectives.* N. Y.: The Free Press.

WILCOX, R. C., 1971. *The Psychological Consequences of Being a Black American: A Sourcebook of Research by Black Psychologists.* New York: Wiley.

WILKINSON, C. B., 1970. Review of *Black Suicide. American Journal of Psychiatry*, 127:177-178.

WILSON, D. C. and E. M. LANTZ, 1957. The effect of culture change on the Negro race in Virginia as indicated by a study of state hospital admissions. *American Journal of Psychiatry*, 114:25-32.

WISPE, L., J. AWKWARD, M. HOFFMAN, P. ASH, L. H. HICKS, and J. PORTER, 1969. The Negro psychologist in America. *American Psychologist*, 24:142-150.

WITMER, A. H., 1891. Insanity in the colored race in the United States. *Alienist and Neurologist*, 12:19-30.

WOLFF, P. H., 1970. "Critical Periods" in human cognitive development. *Hospital Practice*, 5:77-87.

WOOD, F. G., 1968. *Black Scare: The Racist Response to Emancipation and Reconstruction.* Berkeley: University of California Press.

YERKES, R. M., 1921. Psychological examining in the United States Army. National Academy of Sciences, *Memoir*, XV.

ZILBOORG, G., 1941. *A History of Medical Psychology.* N. Y.: Norton.

Index

Abrahamsen, D., 104-105, 159
Ackerman, N. W., 85, 159
Adams, J. Q., 18
Adams, P. L., 143, 159
Adolescence (Hall), 7
Adorno, T. W. 118-119, 159
Agassiz, L., 3
Aggression, 116-117
Alexander, F. G., 58, 159
Allport, G. W., 14-15, 117, 159
Altop, L., 159
American Dilemma, An (Myrdal), 111 fn.
American Journal of Insanity, 12, 19
American Journal of Psychiatry, 11, 12
American Journal of Psychology, 7
American Orthopsychiatric Association, 146
American Psychiatric Association, 127, 146-147
American Psychoanalytic Association, 135
American Psychological Association, 146, 149
American Racism (Daniels and Kitano, 113
Anastasi, A., 35, 39, 159
Andrews, J. B., 20, 159
Anger, as response to oppression, 53-54, 62-63, 66, 95
Anna Karenina (Tolstoy), 84
Anxiety, 62, 105, 124, 125
  stress and, 48
Army Alpha and Beta tests, 35, 36-37
Aronson, H., 135, 170
"Aryan" supremacy, doctrine of, 24 fn.
Ash, P., 170
Athon, J., 18 fn.
Auerbach, H. A., 76, 168
Authoritarian personality, 118-119
Awkward, J., 170

Babcock, C. G., 60-61, 62fn., 165
Babcock, J. W., 20, 128, 159
Bahn, A. K., 138, 159
Bandler, B., 156, 159
Baratz, J. C., 72, 73, 76, 159
Baratz, S. S., 72, 73, 76, 159
Bateson, G., 94
Bayley, N., 80, 160
Bayton, J. A., 149, 160
Bean, R. B., 4-5, 160
Bear, R., 164
Behavioral Genetics, 28-30
Beiser, H. R., 84, 160
Benedict, R., 37, 160
Berkeley-Hill, O. A. R., 104, 160
Berlin, I. N., 156, 160
Bernard, J., 86, 160
Bernard, L. L., 14, 160
Bernard, V. W., 143, 155-156, 160
Bernstein, B., 69-70, 160
Bevis, W. M., 11-12, 128, 129, 160
Billingsley, A., 45, 59, 87, 89, 100, 160
Binet, A., 34
Birch, H. G., 78, 160
Bird, B., 117 fn., 160
Black Bourgeoisie (Frazier), 90
Black Families in White America (Billingsley), 45
Black liberation movement, v, 51, 56, 95, 106
Black Rage (Grier and Cobbs), 54-55
Black Scholar, The, 55
Black Suicide (Hendin), 132
Blacks, Medical Schools, and Society (Curtis), 147
Blauner, R., 58, 160
Bleuler, E., 110, 124 fn., 160
Bloom, B. S., 79-80, 160
Boas, F., 5, 26, 30
Bradford, R., 109
Branham, E., 99, 160
Brigham, C. C., 36, 160, 161
Brill, A. A., 14

171

Brody, E. B., 59, 92-93, 94, 161, 167
Brophy, J., 164
Brown, L. L., 50 fn., 161
Brown, S., 109, 161
Butler, J. S., 18 fn.
Butts, H. F., 54-55, 142 fn., 151, 152, 153, 161, 164, 168

Cahoon, D. D., 75, 170
Calhoun, J. C., 17, 18-19
California Personality Inventory, 98
Calnek, M., 142 fn., 161
Cartwright, S., 2
Caste and Class in a Southern Town (Dollard), 117
Cazden, C., 73, 161
Census of 1840, 16-19
Chamberlain, H. S., 16 fn.
Chandler, C. A., 159
Chess, S., 63, 92, 161
Children of Crisis (Coles), 77
Chomsky, N., 74
Cicero, 23
Civil rights movement, 124
Clark, K. B., xi, 47, 52, 53, 63, 69, 131, 161
Clark, M. P., 53, 161
Cobbs, P. M., 54-55, 91, 95, 142 fn., 163
Coles, R., 51fn., 77, 161
Collins, C. W., 49 fn., 50 fn., 161
Color blindness, 29
  illusion of, 57-66, 142
Comer, J. P., 44, 114, 154-155, 161
Compensatory Education, 40-41, 68
Comprehensive Textbook of Psychiatry (Freedman and Kaplan), 58
Confessions of Nat Turner, The (Styron), 102
Critical periods hypothesis, 79-80
Cronbach, L. J., 32 fn., 42, 161
Crow, J., 39-40, 161
Cultural deprivation, 47, 67-82
Culturally Deprived Child, The (Riessman), 67
Culture, black, 58-59, 65
"Culture of poverty" hypothesis, 71-72, 80-81
"Culture-free" tests, 38-39
Curtis, J. L., 147, 148, 161

Dain, N., 18 fn., 127 fn., 162
Daniels, R., 113, 162
Dark Ghetto (Clark), 52
Darwin, C., 6
Davenport, C. B., 109, 162
Davidson, H. H., 73-74, 162
"Deficit" model, 67-82

Defoe, D., 110
Dementia praecox, 9, 12
Depression, 128-131
Deprivation, cultural, 47, 67-82
Derbyshire, R. L., 168
Desegregation, 124, 147
Detroit, race riots in, 115
Deutsch, A., 18, 162
Deutsch, M., 32 fn., 162
Diesenhaus, H., 157, 168
Divorce rates, 85, 86
Dobzhansky, T., 33-34, 110, 162, 167
Dollard, J., 116-117, 119, 162
Doob, L. W., 162
"Double-bind" theory, 94
Dovenmuehle, R. H., 130, 162
Drapetomania, 2
Draw-a-Man Test, 39
Dreams, blacks and, 9-11
Dryman, I., 169
Du Bois, W. E. B., 5, 21, 103, 162
Dunham, H. W., 123, 162
Dunn, L. C., 110, 162
Dysaesthesia Aethiopica, 2

Education, medical, 147-149
Ehrlich, P. H., 110, 162
Einstein, A., 120
Eisenberg, L., 159
Ellison, R., 46, 162
English, W. T., 102
Entwisle, D. R., 73, 162
Epidemiology, 16-20, 122-134
Equality, concept of, 33-34
Essay on the Inequality of Human Races (Gobineau), 24 fn.
Eugenics, 43
Evarts, A. B., 8-9, 162
Evolutionary lag, 6-14
Exploitation, psychological, 114
"Extinction" thesis, 21
Eysenck, H. J., 33, 162

Family, 83-100
Fanon, F., 59, 112, 141, 162
Faris, R., 123, 162
Farley, R., 86, 162
Fernandez, P., 169
Fischer, J., 123, 162
Ford, C. S., 162
Foundations of the Nineteenth Century, The (Chamberlain), 16 fn.
Frazier, F., vi, 90
Freedman, A. M., 58, 162
Freedman, D. X., 58, 168
Frenkel-Brunswik, E., 159
Freud, S., 7, 7fn., 10, 11, 14, 60, 116, 120, 163

Fried, M. H., 30, 163
Friedberg, B., 166
Frumkin, R. M., 163
"Frustration-aggression" hypothesis, 116-117
Fuller, J. L., 28, 163

Gardner, E. A., 159
Garrett, H. E., 30, 163
Gearhart, L. P., 105, 163
Genetic fallacy, the, 23-44
George, W. C., 30
Ginsberg, M., 121, 163
Glazer, N., 59, 81, 163
Gobineau, Count de, 24 fn.
Goldstein, N. F., 107, 163
Goodenough, F. L., 38-39, 163
Gordon, E. W., 41, 163
Gordon, J. E., 78, 163
Gossett, T. F., 29 fn., 42 fn., 163
Grant, M., 24 fn.
Grapes of Wrath, The (Steinbeck), 84
Greenberg, J. W., 73-74, 162
Grier, W. H., 54-55, 91, 95, 142 fn., 163
Gross, H. S., 64, 128, 163
Grossack, M. M., 163
Gullattee, A. C., 45, 134, 163
Gurin, P., 165
Gussow, J. D., 78, 160

Hall, G. S., 3, 7, 163, 164
Haller, J. S., 21, 102, 103, 164
Ham, Curse of, 1-2, 95
Hamburg, D. A., 135, 164
Hamilton, J. W., 116, 164
Hannerz, U., 46, 164
Hansberry, L., 94
Harlem, 46, 98, 131
Harris, D. B., 39, 163
Harris, M., 5, 7, 27, 164
Harrison, P. A., 151, 152, 153, 164
Harwood, E., 166
Head Start, 40, 68
Health and Nutrition, 78-79
Health and Physique of the North American Negro, The (Du Bois), 5
Hemingway, E., 78
Hendin, H., 132-133, 164
Henson, J., 88, 164
Hermalin, A. I., 86, 162
Hernton, C. C., 103, 164
Hertzig, M. E., 169
Herzog, E., 89, 91, 98, 99, 153, 154, 164
Hess, R. D., 70, 164
Hicks, L. H., 170

Higham, J., 43, 164
Hill, R. B., 91 fn.
Hirsh, J., 28, 164
History of the Negro in Medicine, The (Morais), 18 fn.
Hitler, A., 112
Hocking, F., 47, 164
Hoffman, M., 170
Hollingshead, A. B., 122, 164
Holm, R. W., 110, 162
Houston, S. H., 74-76, 165
Hovland, C. K., 162
Howard, J., 166
Howe, S. G., 18 fn.
Hughes, L., 94
Hunt, J. McV., 70, 77, 165
Hunter, D. M., 60-61, 62 fn., 165

Illegitimacy, 85, 86, 87
Illinois Test of Psycholinguistic Abilities, 75 fn.
Indians, American, 29
Inequality, 33-34
Inferiority, black, premise of, 1-22, 23-44, 52, 102, 124, 125
Instinct Hypothesis, 14-16, 26
Institutionalization of racism, v, 76, 113, 137
Intelligence tests, blacks and, 30-44
Intermarriage, 107-111
Interpretation of Dreams, The (Freud), 10
Introduction to Social Psychology (McDougall), 15
IQ tests, 30-44
Irish, prejudice against, 126 fn.

Jaco, E. G., 123, 165
Jacobson, L., 76, 168
Jarvis, E., 17, 18, 19, 165
Jaspers, K., 124 fn., 165
Jefferson, T., 102
Jeliffe, S. E., 8
Jensen, A. R., xiii, 25-26, 30-34, 154, 165
Jews, 16 fn., 36, 43, 114
Johnson, C. S., vi
Joint Commission on Mental Health of Children, 86, 165
Jones, B. E., 136, 137, 150, 165
Jordan, W. D., 102, 165
Jung, C. G., 13-14, 165

Kagan, J. S., 40-41, 165
Kaplan, H. I., 58, 162
Kaplan, S., 111, 165
Kardiner, A., 48-52, 54, 55, 56, 62, fn., 103, 132, 165

Karno, M., 63-64, 165
Katz, I., 165
Kennedy, J., 55-56, 165
Kipling, R., 7
Kitano, H., 113, 162
Klee, G., 123, 165, 167
Kleiner, R., 133, 134, 166, 167
Klerman, G. L., 170
Klineberg, O., 36, 166
Knowles, L. L., 166
Kolb, L. C., 58, 166
Kovel, J., 105, 119-120, 166

Labov, W., 72, 166
Ladner, J. A., 89, 96, 166
Lamarckianism, 25 fn.
Language, 69-77
Lantz, E. M., 125, 126, 127, 170
Le Bon, G., 24, 166
Lee, E. S., 133, 167
Lenneberg, E., 74
Levinson, D. J., 159
Lewis, H., 80-81, 89, 91, 98, 164, 166
Lewis, O., 69, 71-72, 166
Liberation movement, black, v, 51, 56, 95, 166
Lidz, T., 58, 88, 166
Life and Confessions of a Psychologist (Hall), 7
Light, R. E., 167
Lightfoot, O. B., 165
Lincoln, C. E., 57, 166
Lind, J. E., 9-10, 166
Lindzey, G., 30, 169
Litwack, L. F., 17, 166
Livingstone, F. R., 26, 166
Los Angeles County Department of Adoptions, 99
Lydston, G. F., 103
Lynching, 16, 115

McCarthy, J. D., 35 fn., 166
McCord, W., 96, 166
McDill, E. L., 55 fn., 166
McDougall, W., 15, 166
McGough, W. E., 130, 162
McGurk, F., 30, 166
McLean, H. V., 62, 63, 123, 166

Mahler, M., 61
Mal de mère syndrome, 92
Malinowski, B., 59
Mall, F. P., 5, 166
Malzberg, B., 123, 133, 166, 167
Mankind Evolving (Dobzhansky), 33
Mark of Oppression, The (Kardiner and Ovesey), 48-52, 62 fn., 93, 132
Marriages, interracial, 107-111

Martin, J., 168
Matriarchy, 87-100
May, A. J., 37
Mead, M., 167
Measurement of Intelligence, The (Terman), 35
Medical Schools, 146-149
Mental illness, blacks and, 16-21, 122-145
Metzger, L. P., 113 fn., 167
Meyers, E. D., Jr., 166
Migration and Mental Disorder, 133-134
Miller, N. E., 162
Minnesota Multiphasic Inventory, 97-98
"Miscegenation," 107-111
Modern Clinical Psychiatry, 58
Momism, 91
Monogamy, 6
Monroe, R. R., 167
Montagu, A., 5, 26, 167
Morais, H. M., 18, 167
Morton, S. G., 4
Mothers, black, 87-100
Mowrer, O. H., 162
Moynihan, D. P., 59, 81, 84-85, 87, 89, 90, 163
Moynihan Report, 84-90, 168
My Face Is Black (Lincoln), 57
Myrdal, G., 58, 111 fn., 167
Myths, 1-22, 86, 109, 114, 123

National Center for Health Statistics, 131
National Committee for Mental Hygiene, 43
National Institute of Mental Health, 127, 146-147
National Origins Quota Law, 43
National Urban League, 90 fn.
Nazis, 24 fn., 42, 43
Neel, J. V., 27, 167
Negro Family, The; The Case for National Action (Moynihan), 84, 168
Newby, I. A., 16, 167
Newton, P., 53, 168
Noah, 1
Noble, J. L., 95, 167
Nolen, C. H., 167
"Nordic" supremacy, doctrine of, 24 fn.
North Carolina Patriots, Inc., 30
Northup, S., 22, 167
Notes on Virginia (Jefferson), 102
Nott, J. C., 4

Oedipus complex, 115, 119

INDEX

O'Malley, M., 12-13, 128, 167
Oppression, marks of, 45-56
Our Violent Society (Abrahamsen), 104
Ovesey, L., 48-52, 54, 55, 62 fn., 103, 132, 165

Palmer, D., 165
Paranoia, 54, 58
Parker, S., 133, 134, 166, 167
Pasamanick, B., 126, 128, 167
Passing of the Great Race, The (Grant), 24 fn.
Passow, A. H., 167
Patient services, need for upgrading of, 155-157
Patients, black psychiatric, 135-145
Patriarchies, 90
Paykel, E. S., 170
Perry, C., 73, 169
Person, The (Lidz), 88
Personality, authoritarian, 118-119
Pettigrew, T. F., 97, 126 fn., 128 fn., 167
Physical decline theory, 21
Pierce, C. M., 148-149, 155, 167
Porter, J., 170
Postell, W. D., 20, 167
Poussaint, A. F., 102, 168
Poverty, 67-82
  family breakdown and, 86-87
Prange, A. J., 128, 129, 132, 168
Prejudice, 117, 117 fn., 118
  effects of, 53
  roots of, 112-121
Prewitt, K., 166
Proshansky, H., 53, 168
Pseudo-transference, 144
Psychiatrists, black, need for, 147, 148, 151
Psychiatry
  black patients and, 135-145
  challenge to profession of, 146-157
Psychoanalytical Review, The, 8, 9, 11
Psychology of Peoples, The (Le Bon), 24
Psychotherapy, family, 83
Putnam, C., 30
Pygmalion in the Classroom (Rosenthal and Jacobson), 76

Quarles, B., 45, 168

Race and Reason (Putnam), 30
Race Crossing in Jamaica (Davenport), 109, 162
Races of Mankind, The (Benedict and Weltfish), 37
Rage, 48, 53-54

Rainwater, L., 84, 168
Raisin in the Sun, A (Hansberry), 94
Redlich, F. C., 58, 122, 164, 168
Referral Procedures, 151-153
Research, 153-155
Riessman, F., 67, 168
Rigsby, L., 166
Riots, race, 115-117
Roberts, O. S., 160
Robinson, H. A., 118 fn., 168
Rodman, H., 80, 168
Roosevelt, T., 8, 43
Rosenthal, R., 76, 168
Rush, B., vi, vii, 168
Ryan, W., 81-82, 85, 168

Sabshin, M., 137, 157, 168
Sanford, R. N., 159
Said of Toledo, 23
"Scapegoat" hypothesis, 117
Schachter, J. S., 142 fn., 168
Schleifer, C. B., 138, 168
Schultz, C. B., 76, 168
Schuster, D. B., 105, 163
Schizophrenia, 94, 122, 123, 127, 128
School Achievers from a Deprived Background (Davidson and Greenberg), 73
Sclare, A., 95, 97, 168
Sears, R. R., 162
Segregation, 16, 47
Selesnick, S., 58, 159
Self-esteem, black, 49-56
Services, patient, need for upgrading of, 155-157
Sex identity, 97-99
Sexuality, 101-111
Shaler, N. S., 24-25, 168
Sharpley, R. H., 60, 168
Shipman, V. C., 164
Shockley, W., 42-43, 168
Shuey, A., 30, 168
Sickle cell trait, 29
Siegel, N. H., 135, 169
Sigel, I. E., 73, 169
Simon, R. I., 123, 169
Simon, T., 34
Simpson, G. E., 53, 169
Slobin, D. I., 73, 169
Smith, J. McC., 18
Snow, J., 122
Social Class and Mental Illness (Hollingshead and Redlich), 122
Social Darwinism, 25 fn.
Sollenberger, R. T., 162
Spencer, H., 6
Spuhler, J. N., 30, 169
Spurlock, J., 53, 169

Stability and Change in Human Characteristics (Bloom), 79
Stampp, K. M., 2, 3, 21, 88, 169
Stanton, W., 3, 4, 169
Staples, R., 89, 96, 103, 169
Steinbeck, J., 84
Sterba, R., 115, 119, 169
Stereotypes, vi, 9, 11, 13, 23, 29, 52, 55 fn., 63, 66, 72, 76, 86, 92, 96, 100, 102, 103, 109, 128, 131, 143
Sterilization, 43
Stewart, W., 72, 169
Stocking, G. W., Jr., 25 fn., 169
Stowe, H. B., 88
Strengths of Black Families, The, 90 fn.
Stress, 47-49
Styron, W., 102
Sudia, C. E., 98, 99, 164
Suicide, 131-133
Sullivan, H. S., vi-vii, 169
Supervisors, training institute, 150-151
Szwed, J. F., 170

"Tangle of pathology" thesis, 87-88
TenHouten, W., 89, 92, 169
Terman, L. M., 34-35, 169
Tests, intelligence, blacks and, 30-44
Textbooks, psychiatric, 58
This Side of Jordan (Bradford), 109
Thomas, A., 38, 63, 144, 161, 169
Thomas, W. I., 16, 170
Thompson, W. R., 28, 163
Thorndike, E. L., 7 fn., 42 fn.
Tobach, E., 167
Tobias, P. V., 5, 170
Tolstoy, L., 84
Tomorrow's Tomorrow: The Black Woman (Ladner), 96
Tonks, C. M., 131, 170
Training Programs, 150-151
Transference, 144

Valentine, C. A., 81, 89, 170
Vincent, C., 98, 170
Violence, racist, 115
Vitols, M. M., 123, 128, 129, 130, 132, 168

Waddell, K. J., 75, 170
War, 120
Washburn, S. L., 26, 170
Watts, 96
Weatherly, U. G., 16, 170
Weaver, W. A., 19
Weintraub, W., 135, 170
Weltfish, G., 37, 160
Wexberg, E., 128, 170
Wharton, E., 84
White, J., 65, 170
White, W. A., 8, 124 fn., 170
White Citizens' Councils, 30
White Racism: A Psychohistory (Kovel), 119-120, 166
Whitten, N. E., 170
Wilcox, R. C., 170
Wilkerson, D. A., 41, 163
Wilkerson, R. G., 157, 165, 168
Wilkinson, C. B., 133 fn., 170
Williams, D. H., 165
Williams, R. K., 160
Wilson, D. C., 124, 125, 126, 170
Wilson, J. S., 3
Wispé, L., 149, 170
Witmer, A. H., 20, 170
Wolff, P. H., 79, 170
Women, black, 87-100, 102
Wood, F. G., 11, 170
Woodworth, R., 29

Yancey, W. L., 55 fn., 84, 166, 168
Yerkes, R. M., 35-36, 170
Yinger, J. M., 53, 169
Young, W., 154 fn.

Zilboorg, G., 58, 170

1